FEARLESS CAPTAIN

THE ADVENTURES OF

JOHN SMITH

FEARLESS CAPTAIN

THE ADVENTURES OF

JOHN SMITH

Aleck Loker

MORGAN REYNOLDS

PUBLISHING

Greensboro, North Carolina

Founders of the Republic

John Smith

John Paul Jones

Alexander Hamilton

Andrew Jackson

John Adams

Dolley Madison

Thomas Jefferson

Sam Houston

FEARLESS CAPTAIN: THE ADVENTURES OF JOHN SMITH

Copyright © 2006 by Aleck Loker

Library of Congress Cataloging-in-Publication Data

Loker, Aleck.
    Fearless captain : the adventures of John Smith / Aleck Loker.— 1st ed.
        p. cm.
Includes bibliographical references and index.
    ISBN-13: 978-1-931798-83-9 (library binding)
    ISBN-10: 1-931798-83-4 (library binding)
    1. Smith, John, 1580-1631—Juvenile literature. 2.
Colonists—Virginia—Jamestown—Biography—Juvenile literature. 3.
Explorers—America—Biography—Juvenile literature. 4. Explorers—Great
Britain—Biography—Juvenile literature. 5. Jamestown (Va.)—History—17th
century—Juvenile literature. 6. Jamestown (Va.)—Biography—Juvenile
literature. 7. Virginia—History—Colonial period, ca. 1600-1775—Juvenile
literature. I. Title.
    F229.S7L65 2006
    973.2'1092—dc22

                                    2005032442

Printed in the United States of America
First Edition

To Thad Tate,
for all his advice and assistance
with the manuscript

CONTENTS

A NOTE ON SOURCES

For a century, historians viewed John Smith's reported exploits as the exaggerations of a braggart, perhaps one who had bitter memories of his treatment by some of the Virginia Company leaders. However, we now know that John Smith wrote truthfully and, at times, humbly about all he experienced. This knowledge comes from the extensive research of Philip Barbour and others, particularly historians in eastern Europe, who have verified it. Philip Barbour published his research over a thirty-year period ending in the 1980s. Barbour's finest tribute to Captain John Smith consists of three volumes—*The Complete Works of Captain John Smith,* with extensive editorial notations by Barbour.

John Smith. (Courtesy of the Granger Collection.)

one
BORN TO
ESCAPE

In a longhouse at Werowocomoco, in what is now coastal Virginia, John Smith struggled as four Native-American warriors forced him to the ground and pinioned him, pushing his head roughly onto a flat stone. He tried to break free, but each man held one of his arms or legs in a powerful grip.

Each of the forty or so men in the longhouse stood quite tall—six feet or more. They had painted their faces and shoulders red. Some had covered their heads with white goose down; others wore coronets of feathers. An equal number of women stood in a row parallel to the men. They also wore the red paint, and many had long strings of large white pearls around their necks. They wore little clothing even though the sole fire pit provided meager comfort from the frigid winter storm outside.

For the previous three days, seven shamans had conducted a ritual of dancing and chanting while constructing intricate designs of sticks and corn on the floor of the longhouse. They had painted their faces black and red, with ghostly white paint around their eyes giving them a devilish appearance. They wore stuffed skins of snakes and weasels around their heads, necks, and shoulders, and they shook gourd rattles. From the little bit of their language that Smith had learned, he understood that their ritual would reveal whether they should consider him a friend or an enemy. When the ceremony had ended, they did not tell Smith their conclusion.

Instead, they had brought him to the largest longhouse in the encampment, where Powhatan, the leader of all the Native Americans in tidewater Virginia, sat on his throne, draped in a long robe made from raccoon skins, his winter garb. Powhatan sat with two young women at his side while one of the shamans spoke. At the end of the shaman's speech, with no apparent signal from Powhatan, the four warriors grabbed Smith and forced him to the ground.

As he lay there, his fate became apparent. A fifth warrior stepped forward with a wooden club in his hand. Smith had seen the terrible effect of these war clubs in previous skirmishes with Powhatan's men.

What happened next is the stuff of legend, described in numerous ways. Pocahontas came to the rescue, and Smith's life was spared. The adventurous captain would live to see

The Country wee now call Virginia beginneth at Cape Henry distant from Roanoack 60 miles, where was Sr Walter Raleigh's plantation: and because the people differ very little from them of Powhatan in any thing, I have inserted those figures in this place because of the conveniency.

King Powhatan comands C. Smith to be slayne, his daughter Pokahontas beggs his life his thankfullnes and how he subiected 39 of their kings. reade y history.

printed by James Reeve

This colorized image from John Smith's 1624 "Generall Historie of Virginia" depicts the scene during which Powhatan decided the captain's fate. (Courtesy of the Granger Collection.)

more escapades, as he had grown used to experiencing for most of his life.

15

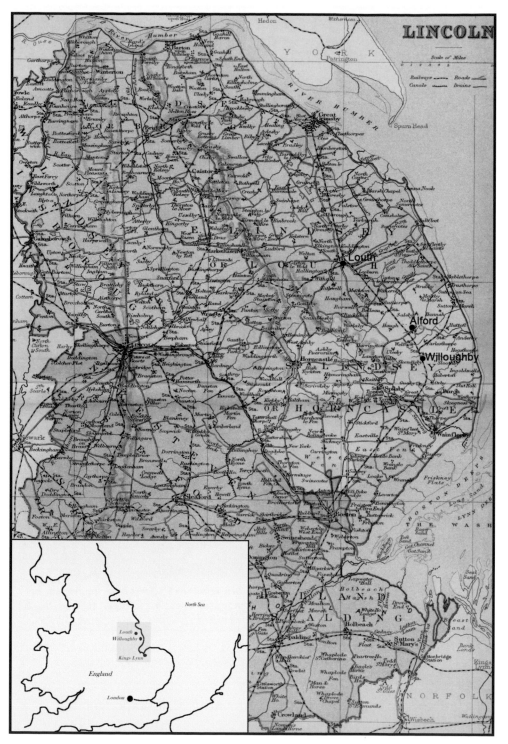

Lincolnshire, the British county of Smith's childhood, and the region from which he longed to escape. (Library of Congress)

On January 9, 1580, George and Alice Smith baptized their firstborn son, John, at St. Helena's Church in Willoughby, Lincolnshire, England. Willoughby sits only five or six miles west of the North Sea shore. The village takes its name from the lords Willoughby, whose family name was Bertie. John Smith's father, George, was a yeoman farmer who rented land from Peregrine Bertie, then Lord Willoughby, who was a decorated soldier in Elizabethan England. George Smith was not on the lowest rung of the social ladder but was near the bottom. He owned property in Lincolnshire and must have been moderately successful. George's father, for whom John was named, had also owned property—perhaps the same land that passed to George and then to his grandson. In addition to Lord Willoughby being George Smith's landlord, the Smith family was also connected to the Berties through marriage. This family connection would be important to John throughout his life.

John Smith came into a world of exciting times. Spain, France, and England dominated western Europe between 1580 and 1600. The Low Countries (present-day Netherlands, Belgium, Luxembourg, and northwest France) were partitioned, with Spain controlling the southern half and the northern half governed as the United Provinces. England and France, traditional rivals, shared the desire to eject Spain from the Netherlands.

In central and eastern Europe, a number of small states—such as Bavaria, Saxony, and Venice—supported the Holy Roman Empire in its opposition to the Ottoman Empire that controlled much of eastern Europe, including modern-day Romania, Bulgaria, and parts of Hungary. This high period of the "Age of Exploration" saw Spain, England, Portugal, France, and the Netherlands contending for dominance in various parts of the world. In 1602, the Netherlands formed the East India Company. Spain had already established solid outposts in the Americas, and England had made several failed attempts to establish a foothold in North America, most notably the "lost colony" planted at Roanoke Island.

Smith spent his infancy in Willoughby. The Smiths looked to larger villages in Lincolnshire for John's education. Early on, he traveled three miles to Alford, where he attended the tiny Queen Elizabeth I Grammar School located above St. Wilfrid's Church. Later, he enrolled at the Free Grammar School of King Edward VI, twenty-three miles across flat and marshy land in Louth. At both schools he studied the usual grammar school subjects of that time: reading, writing, arithmetic, and Latin—the same education William Shakespeare would have received.

The eastern Lincolnshire countryside of endless cultivated fields, gently rolling hills, and fertile marshes must have seemed boring to an imaginative boy who had heard tales of Sir Francis Drake, Sir Walter Raleigh, and other seagoing adventurers. Five years after the Spanish Armada's unsuccessful attack on England, John, then

Sir Francis Drake, British navigator, privateer, explorer, and politician. (National Portrait Gallery, London)

thirteen, sold his satchel and books, secretly intending to go to sea. However, his father discovered John's plan and put a stop to it.

Two years later, his father arranged for John to serve as an apprentice under Thomas Sendall of King's Lynn on

The Norman town of Le Havre, located in northwest France along the English Channel, was one of France's largest and most active ports during Smith's lifetime. (Musée des Beaux Artes, Le Havre)

the Great Ouse River, which flowed into the North Sea. King's Lynn is sixty miles from Willoughby—a three-day journey. Sendall was a prosperous merchant, and George may have believed that John's interest in the sea could find an outlet by working with Sendall. But John soon found that Sendall expected him to stay on shore and attend to the tedium of the mercantile business. He ran away from King's Lynn at age fifteen.

George Smith died in the spring of the next year, 1596. As the eldest son, John inherited a small estate valued at about seventy-seven pounds sterling—approximately $18,000 today. Since John was not yet of legal age to manage his own affairs, his estate was placed under the management of a guardian, George Metham, a friend of Lord Willoughby.

Nonetheless, John intended to travel and see the world. So, in 1596, at the age of sixteen, with a small sum of money from his guardians (ten shillings, equal to $114 now), John set off for London. From London, John traveled to Rouen in France. His money soon spent, he traveled down the Seine River to Le Havre, where he enlisted in the army in an English company under Captain Duxbury. Joseph Duxbury had earlier served under Lady Willoughby's first cousin, Sir Francis Vere. In joining this English company, John emulated Lord Willoughby, one of his role models. Captain Duxbury's company was engaged in England's continued drive to eject Spain from the Low Countries and to prevent their meddling in French affairs. Thus began John's military career at the age of sixteen. Under Captain Duxbury in the Netherlands and France, John Smith undertook the task of mastering the skills of armed combat and horsemanship.

two
FIRST
TASTE OF
ADVENTURE

With Captain Duxbury's guidance, John Smith learned how to use firearms, how to fight with swords in the melee of the battlefield, and how to move in battle formation as part of a company rather than as an individual. He received some training in practice sessions, but most of his skill came from the frightening exposure to actual, and almost immediate, combat. Those who survived learned quickly from their experiences; those who had not died.

Warfare at this time involved horsemen and foot soldiers formed into ranks fighting in close quarters. A soldier's choices for weaponry were varied: lances, pikes, swords, daggers, muskets, pistols, axes, and bows and arrows. Armies also included artillery companies that fired cannons. The cannons had two main functions: to

Soldiers battle outside the fortified European city of Bruges in this Renaissance-era painting by Jean Froissart. (Courtesy of Art Resource.)

breach defensive walls and to fire at troops on the battlefield. The lance or pike was a slender hardwood pole, often ten to fifteen feet long, tipped with a long tapered steel point. Foot soldiers as well as horsemen carried these weapons. Behind the pikemen, soldiers armed with muskets or harquebuses (a large heavy gun often positioned on a support) fired at the approaching enemy troops.

Although flintlock muskets had been invented by this time, most musketeers or harquebusiers still carried the older and less expensive matchlock weapons, whose charge was ignited by a slow-burning match lowered over a hole in the gun's breech. Horsemen carried a variety of arms, including pistols, muskets, lances, and swords. Their mobility and elevation above the foot soldiers gave them an advantage. When a horseman lost his horse in battle, he found himself in great peril at ground level among the swirling, hacking, and thrusting opponents.

A soldier's life consisted of low pay (about ten shillings per month), harsh living conditions, and constant danger. Soldiers typically stripped the countryside of livestock and other food as they foraged for their own survival in a hostile land. When troops captured a rich town or fortification, they seized any valuables for themselves. They respected the rule of force much more than the rule of law. John Smith would have realized quickly that to command respect in the army, he would have to seize control by the force of his will and his physical ability.

By 1598, the Spanish had signed the Treaty of Vervins, and hostilities with France ended. With the war over, Smith returned to Willoughby, a young man of eighteen with some military experience. But his wanderlust was far from satisfied. In 1599, he arranged to accompany one of Lord Willoughby's younger sons, also named Peregrine Bertie, to Orleans, France, where Peregrine was to join his older brother, Robert, on a tour of Europe.

After he successfully united the brothers in Orleans, Smith received sufficient funds to return to England.

However, he decided to remain in France for a while. In Paris he met a friend of the Willoughbys, David Hume, a poet and distant cousin of a prominent Scotsman. Hume helped Smith spend the money the Berties had paid him, and in return Smith got letters of reference to introduce him to the court of King James of Scotland.

With his funds depleted, Smith embarked on a ship bound for Scotland, intending to seek his fortune. His ship wrecked en route, at the island of Lindisfarne off the coast of England. Smith became ill and remained on Lindisfarne until he recovered, and then he made his way to Edinburgh, where he presented the letters of introduction Hume had given him. Although he received kind treatment from the Scots, the letters proved worthless. What Smith needed to make connections in the court of King James was money—something he had little of— and so he returned to Willoughby, wiser and more worldly, but still landlocked in Lincolnshire.

Soon tiring of his companions in Lincolnshire— young men who were far more content with the rural life and its endless cycles of tending crops and cattle— Smith moved into a wooded pasture surrounded by a dense forest on the Willoughby estate. There he built a simple shelter of tree boughs by a small stream and began a hermit's life. He studied Machiavelli's *Art of War* and read the works of the Roman philosopher Marcus Aurelius. He also practiced jousting with a horse and lance, using a ring as a target.

Smith learned from Marcus Aurelius the signficance

Niccolò Machiavelli, born in Florence, Italy in 1469, was a political philosopher whose ideas about statesmanship, politics, and power dramatically influenced the development of Renaissance leaders. (Palazzo Vecchio, Florence)

of having a strong commitment to self-control, a commitment to hard work, and perhaps most importantly, the value of ambition. Marcus Aurelius advised in book four of his *Meditations,* "Let no act be done without a purpose, nor otherwise than according to the perfect principles of art." John Smith followed that advice throughout his life; he appears to have had a clear purpose in mind for everything he did.

From Niccolò Machiavelli's *Art of War,* John Smith learned how armies are organized: from the basic fighting unit of a company led by a captain, through battalions, regiments commanded by colonels, and armies led by generals. He learned how armies train to move as units on the battlefield, and how to develop and employ battle tactics. In the appendices to the English translation of Machiavelli's work, he also learned the valuable lessons of sending messages over long distances by using signals, and how to build and employ various types of pyrotechnic (explosive) devices in war.

While in the forest, Smith's diet consisted mainly of venison from the deer that he had hunted himself. Whatever else he needed, a friend brought from the village. His friends, though, became concerned about Smith's lifestyle. They arranged for Signore Theodore Paleologue, an Italian nobleman in the employ of the Earl of Lincoln, to visit Smith. The Italian was an excellent horseman, and with encouragement from Lord Willoughby, convinced Smith to follow him to Tattershall, one of the Earl of Lincoln's estates. There he helped Smith refine his horsemanship skills. Smith probably also learned to speak a bit of Italian then.

Smith possessed an apparent skill in learning languages, and throughout his life his ability to converse with people from many different cultures—Europeans, Asians, Africans, and Native Americans—served him well. Theodore Paleologue may also have exposed Smith to the stories of the Ottoman Empire's subjugation of eastern Europe. It's quite possible that his conversations with Paleologue may have enlightened him about the fierce religious wars consuming eastern Europe, especially those involving the Muslim Turks.

Late in 1600, Smith returned to the Netherlands and then to France, where he intended to find the Duke of Mercoeur and enlist in the Holy Roman Empire's army. Smith wrote that he had tired of Christians killing one another in the wars of western Europe, and he wanted to be part of the Christian attempt to regain eastern Europe from the occupying Turk army.

The French Duke of Mercoeur, Philippe-Emmanuel de Lorraine, was a strange person for Smith to seek out, for the duke had led a treasonous revolt against King Henry IV of France in the late sixteenth century. In league with the Spaniards, this staunch Roman Catholic had opposed Protestant Henry IV in the wars of religion. Consequently, when John Smith fought under Captain Duxbury, Duke Mercoeur was the enemy. Smith may not have been aware of this political irony, since he made no mention of the duke in connection with his service in the previous conflict. The Duke of Mercoeur had capitulated to Henry IV

Philippe-Emmanuel de Lorraine, Duke of Mercoeur. (Library of Congress)

at Angers on March 20, 1598, and received a royal pardon for his treason.

Since that time, Duke Mercoeur had applied his military expertise to the cause of the Holy Roman Empire. He held a position as a general in the multinational army under Emperor Rudolph II in Hungary. Smith hoped to meet the Duke at his home in St. Valery-sur-Somme in the Picardy region of France. On his way, in the winter of 1600, he fell in with four French adventurers who were masquerading as a great nobleman named "Depreau" and his three gentlemen friends.

During a river voyage, the four Frenchmen slipped away from the ship with Smith's trunk and all his belongings. The thieves left him with only the clothes he wore, and Smith had to sell his coat to pay the ship's master for his passage. He soon learned from another soldier he met, a man called Curzianvere, that the so-called Lord Depreau was merely a lawyer's son from Mortain in Brittany. His three accomplices were likewise just con men who duped unsuspecting travelers.

Curzianvere offered to help Smith catch up with Depreau and his cronies to reclaim his property. And so the two soldiers traveled together through Caen. There they visited the priory of St. Steven, where they saw the tomb of William the Conqueror. Continuing on to Mortain, Smith found Depreau, but not compensation.

Dejected and with his meager funds spent, Smith was reduced to sleeping in the forest. A rich French farmer found him there, demoralized and near dead from the bitter cold. The farmer took Smith home and restored his health. As he became stronger, Smith regained his indomitable spirit. When he stumbled upon one of the con men that had robbed him, they drew their swords, and a fierce duel ensued. Smith's skill and experience from his army service carried the day, drawing the con man's confession that he had taken part in the theft of Smith's belongings. Had not local farmers, observing the duel from the safety of a ruined tower, heard that confession, they would have detained Smith for his aggression. That was all the satisfaction Smith could expect though, since the four men had already disposed of his stolen trunk and clothing.

Smith resumed his travels. He journeyed to Rennes, the next major city on his way to the Mediterranean Sea, where he hoped to find a ship that would take him to Italy. From there he could make his way to Austria and the army of the Holy Roman Emperor.

John Smith had little money at this point in his travels and had to make his way as best he could. He followed the roads and rivers in a meandering path south and depended on the generosity of strangers most of the way.

Arriving at the port of Marseille on the Mediterranean coast of France, Smith boarded a ship bound for Italy. Smith described the other passengers as "a rabble of inhuman provincials" of various nationalities. Unfortunately, as soon as the ship sailed a fierce storm struck, forcing the crew to anchor near one of the small islands south of Marseille. Earlier, Smith had fallen in with a group of Roman Catholic pilgrims on their way to Rome. Upon learning that Smith was an English Protestant, they blamed the storm on him, calling him a heretic. They also made disparaging remarks about Queen Elizabeth I. Since they thought the presence of this English heretic had brought God's wrath down on the ship, they solved their dilemma by simply pitching young John Smith into the roiling waves. Whether the storm immediately subsided is not known.

Fortunately, Smith could swim. He made his way to an island where he spent a cold night shivering in his wet clothes. Smith was becoming more comfortable with the hardships of sleeping on the cold ground without cover. He would suffer many such difficulties during his adventurous life.

The next morning, Smith saw two ships that had sought shelter from the storm on the lee side (sheltered from the wind) of the island. He made his way to one of them, and as luck would have it, the captain of the ship was a friend of the Earl of Plouer, an acquaintance from the war in France.

Captain La Roche welcomed Smith aboard his ship and made him comfortable. When the weather improved, La Roche headed across the Mediterranean Sea, passed Corsica and Sardinia on their port (left) side, and sailed through the Gulf of Tunis. From there, they coasted along North Africa to Alexandria, Egypt, where they unloaded their cargo.

Leaving Alexandria, they sailed to the city of Iskenderun (formerly known as Alexandretta) to see what ships were in the harbor. Why La Roche was interested in that is unclear, but his subsequent actions indicate he may have been checking for rich merchant vessels whose cargo he could take into his now-empty ship. The means by which he planned to obtain the cargoes would become clear to Smith in due time.

From Iskenderun, La Roche sailed to Cyprus and along the Greek coast to Rhodes. They lingered in the Greek Isles for several days, then sailed between Corfu and the Cape of Otranto, at the mouth of the Adriatic Sea.

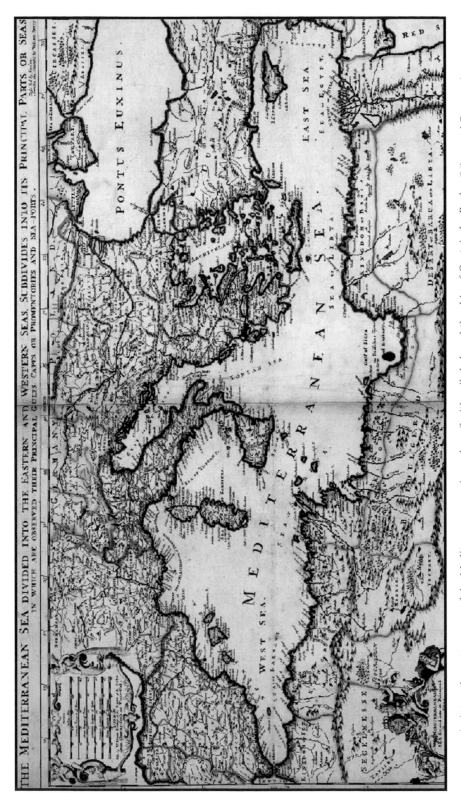

A sixteenth-century map of the Mediterranean region, where Smith sailed aboard the ship of Captain La Roche. (Library of Congress)

There, off the southern tip of Italy, La Roche spied a Venetian merchant ship lumbering out into the Mediterranean Sea. As he maneuvered his ship alongside, La Roche indicated he wanted to speak, but the Venetians mistrusted his intentions and fired a cannon volley, killing one of La Roche's men. La Roche returned fire at the Venetian, then quickly came about so that he could fire his battery of cannons from the other side of the ship.

The Venetian turned tail and attempted to sail out of range of La Roche's cannons, but La Roche pursued him, firing until the Venetian's sails and rigging were destroyed. Having disabled the Venetian, La Roche brought his ship alongside and both ships opened fire on each other. Smith said that the battle continued for one and a half hours. As a final act of desperation, the Venetians set fire to their own ship to keep it out of the Frenchman's hands.

La Roche sent crewmen from his ship over to the Venetian's, and they extinguished the fire. When the Venetian ship began to sink, its captain finally surrendered. La Roche's men then plundered the ship and directed the repairs to the hull to keep it afloat.

The Venetian ship contained an incredible treasure of silk and velvet cloths, and a hoard of gold and silver coins. Smith estimated the Venetian merchant ship to displace about four or five hundred tons—twice the size of La Roche's ship. The Venetian would have been one of the largest merchant ships afloat at that time, and it took La Roche's crew a full day to transfer the cargo. When they had taken all they could, Smith figured the

Venetian ship still contained enough cargo to fill another ship equal in size to La Roche's.

La Roche sailed west toward Sicily to make repairs to his ship, pulling into the harbor of Antibes, Italy. Smith thanked Captain La Roche for his passage to Italy and for the adventures they had shared. For his part in the sea battle, Captain La Roche rewarded Smith with five hundred gold coins, worth about two hundred pounds sterling at that time. Smith's reward would be worth nearly $46,000 today—enough for Smith to live well and travel for several years. La Roche also gave Smith a small box of other valuables worth about the same. Smith had earned a small fortune during his brief service with Captain La Roche and the temptation to stay with the captain from Brittany must have been hard to resist.

During this time, the line between piracy and action taken as a privateer was a fine one, and perhaps nonexistent from a victim's standpoint. A privateer is an armed vessel licensed by a nation with letters of marque, written authorization to seize goods of a foreign state, a portion of which are given to the sponsoring government with the rest kept by the captain and crew. Within a wide definition of piracy, La Roche's actions (and Smith's participation in them) would point to this as a qualifying episode. It was not the only time in Smith's career that he profited through violence and seizure. However, the broad spectrum of Smith's adventures and accomplishments prevents him from being labeled simply as a pirate.

three
THE HOLY
WARS

Smith had made up his mind to join the Christian army in Austria, and as he had demonstrated time and again, he stayed focused on his goal. Leaving La Roche, he began his journey through Italy on his way to Austria. He probably bought a horse and made his way on horseback, traveling through Tuscany on his way to Rome.

Leaving Rome, Smith traveled down the Tiber River and then along the coast southeast to Naples before heading northwest along the length of central Italy to Venice. Smith boarded a ship in Venice, where he undoubtedly had the good sense not to mention his previous encounter with Venetians, and sailed southeast across the Adriatic Sea. After traveling through Croatia and Slovenia, Smith's journey ended at Graz, in the Styria region of Austria. Graz was the seat of Archduke

Ferdinand of Austria and the headquarters of his army. There, Smith met an Englishman and an Irish Jesuit priest, who helped him make important contacts among the leaders of the army. The Jesuits were eager to restore Roman Catholicism in eastern Europe, so the Irish priest introduced Smith to Baron Hans Jacob Khissl, a general of artillery, and the Earl of Meldritch, with whom Smith enlisted as a soldier in the Christian army.

Europe, with its large consolidated kingdoms, such as the Holy Roman Empire, had quite a different political layout in the late sixteenth century than it does today. (Library of Congress)

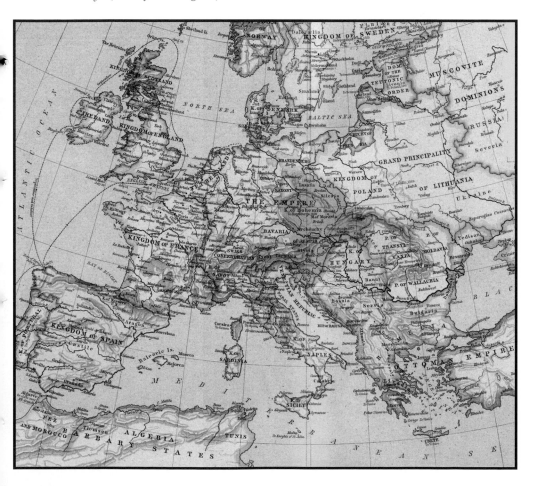

THE HOLY ROMAN EMPIRE

With the coronation of Otto as emperor in 962, the Holy Roman Empire took on a definitive existence as a political entity. The concept of a religious empire came about in 800 when Pope Leo III honored Charlemagne, who took the title of Roman emperor in the West. At first strictly an honorary title, as opposed to having authority over a specific group of people, the title's importance

The coat of arms of the Holy Roman Empire.

eventually developed under Otto, who was the king of Germany at that time. He had pleased the pope by meddling in Italian politics, bringing it under German influence, and received the title as his reward. The German king, who was elected by German princes, usually received the Pope's blessing and was crowned as the Holy Roman Emperor. In certain cases where the German king's ascension was in dispute, the pope might withhold the honor as a show of his power.

The territories and countries held together under the empire included Germany, Austria, Bohemia, Moravia, some of northern Italy, what is now Belgium, the Netherlands, and Switzerland through the middle seventeenth century.

The pope held sway over religious or spiritual matters on Earth, while the Holy Roman Emperor ruled over temporal, or secular, matters affecting Christendom. In theory, all other sovereigns were subservient to the Holy Roman Emperor. In practice, however, the kings and queens of many Christian countries, including England, paid little attention to the Holy Roman Emperor's claim to authority. The king of Germany, and by association the Holy Roman Emperor, became over time less an elected position and more an inherited one. From 1438 until the empire's dissolution in 1806, the crown was in the hands of the Hapsburg dynasty or some related family association.

By Smith's time, the pope's spiritual authority was also not universally accepted. The Reformation in England and within Europe, establishing Protestantism in opposition to Catholicism, had created regions of conflict within the Holy Roman Empire, and the situation was further muddled as conflict with the Muslim Turks heightened. The Empire officially disintegrated when Francis I renounced the post after Napoleon conquered Austria and created a new affiliation of German states.

In Styria, Smith met a man named Ebersbaught, an important military figure. Smith impressed him with his studies of warfare and described to Ebersbaught a way for separated armies to signal to each other using a series of lighted torches, displayed in various patterns of one, two, or three to represent letters of the alphabet.

Sometime later, Ebersbaught found himself and his troops besieged in a fortified city that Smith called Olumpagh (now believed to be Grad in Slovenia). Smith had accompanied Baron Khissl and his army on a march to Olumpagh to liberate the city and Ebersbaught from the controlling Turkish forces. The Turks outnumbered Khissl's army two to one. Storming the city seemed a chancy battle strategy. This gave Smith his first opportunity to prove his mettle in battle.

The Turks had 20,000 men surrounding the hill town of Olumpagh, cutting it off from all conventional means of communication. Smith explained to Baron Khissl how he could send a message to Ebersbaught in the city by the signal-torch method. Under cover of darkness, Khissl's men guided Smith to a hill that overlooked the city about seven miles away.

Using signal torches, Smith sent a message to Ebersbaught that on Thursday night he would lead a charge on the city's east side, and when he made his advance, they should rush out of the city and join in the attack, catching the Turks in a pincer movement, a claw-like convergence of two military forces upon an enemy. Ebersbaught, much to Smith's relief, signaled that the message had been received and understood.

A tributary of the Lendava River passed by Olumpagh and divided the Turkish army into two segments. This situation made Smith's plan more feasible since the river would delay one segment of the Turkish forces from coming to the other's aid. Consequently, the opposing forces were actually more evenly matched, and Khissl had the element of surprise in his favor.

Smith added another clever element to the battle plan, drawn from his studies of warfare. He had Baron Khissl's men tie several thousand pieces of match (fuses for matchlock muskets) to a rope about six hundred feet long. Prior to the attack, they lit the matches, and seeing the burning matches in the night, the Turks assumed the attacking forces were more extensive than they actually were. Further, the diversion allowed Khissl's men to come at the Turks from a different direction. By adding confusion to the Turks side of the equation, the odds tipped in favor of Khissl's men.

When darkness fell, Khissl's 10,000 soldiers launched their attack. Hearing the charge, Ebersbaught led his men out of the city and attacked the Turks from the rear.

About one-third of the Turks died in the battle and many more drowned in the river. The rest fled to Nagykanizsa, a Turkish stronghold well to the southeast.

Baron Khissl placed a garrison of about 2,000 soldiers in Olumpagh to hold the city, then took Smith to Kormend, Hungary, about one day's journey northeast of Olumpagh. As a reward for his clever plan and bravery, Smith received a promotion to the rank of captain and took command of 250 horsemen—a cavalry unit—under the Earl of Meldritch. This promotion to captain remained Smith's proud title throughout his life.

From that time on, he was Captain John Smith.

The dotted lines show Smith's path as a soldier in today's Eastern Europe, from Graz to the battle at Alba Regalis and on to Transylvania.

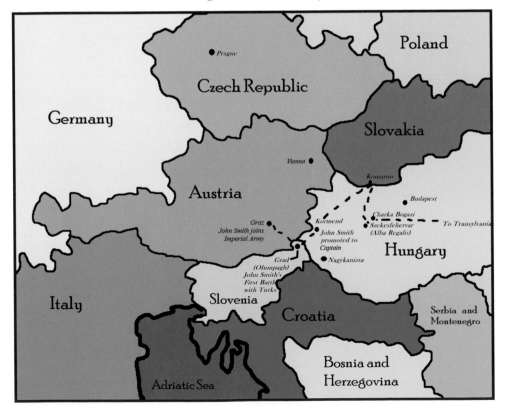

Smith spent the end of the summer of 1601 in Komarno, Slovakia. The Christian army held a fort there near the Danube River. Although Smith heard rumors of a peace between the Christians and the Muslim Turks, they proved false. Instead, the Turks raised additional forces from the various regions they controlled in preparation for aggravated hostilities in the spring.

In response, the emperor formed three armies. One army, led by the emperor's brother, Archduke Mathias, included the French duke Mercoeur—the man Smith had sought unsuccessfully in France. This army was assigned to defend lower Hungary, and Smith initially joined part of that force. A second army, led by Archduke Ferdinand of Styria and the Duke of Mantua, was ordered to capture the city of Nagykanizsa. The third army, under the command of Governor Ferrante Gonzaga of Upper Hungary, along with Giorgio Basta, had orders to run the Turks out of Transylvania.

As part of Meldritch's force, Smith marched with Duke Mercoeur's troops to Alba Regalis (now Szekesfehervar, Hungary) near Lake Balaton, the royal town where the kings of Hungary were crowned and buried. The Turks had captured Alba Regalis in 1543. In 1601, Turks blew up the royal coronation chapel, which contained the graves of Hungarian kings from St. Stephen, who died in 1038, through King John I in 1540.

Duke Mercoeur's forces totaled about 30,000 men of many nationalities (about one-third were French). As a captain, John Smith commanded a company, the most basic of army units. In the army, several companies formed a battalion, commanded by a lieutenant colonel. Several battalions formed a regiment under a colonel; numbers of regiments composed an army under the command of a general. In the case of Emperor Rudolph's forces, at times he had several armies deployed against the Turks. Each army held responsibility for a particular sector or theater of operations, and each had specific defensive or offensive objectives.

Mercoeur's troops laid siege to Alba Regalis, and the Turks soon sallied forth, killing about five hundred Germans under Mercoeur. Then the Turks quickly retreated to the fortified city. The next night, the Turks attacked again, killing an equal number of Hungarians and Bohemians while taking eight to nine hundred French prisoners.

Mercoeur's army needed a better battle strategy. Smith proposed a way to cause panic and confusion within the fortified city. He had demonstrated some explosive devices to Meldritch and other officers during their winter encampment. He proposed to use those devices in the capture of Alba Regalis.

Some Christians who had escaped from the city told the army that the Turks assembled in large numbers for prayer at various times during the day. Smith planned to bombard the city with his explosives when the Turks were assembled, thus causing maximum disruption and casualties. When his plan was approved, Smith filled large earthenware pots with a mixture of gunpowder, musket balls, sulfur, and turpentine. He sealed the pots with cloth and tar after inserting a fuse into each.

These rudimentary bombs worked like modern explosives but with limited power due to the gunpowder available at that time. The powder, packed tightly and constrained by the walls of the ceramic pots, when ignited by the burning fuse, would generate a hot, high-pressure gas that would expand rapidly and explode the pot, sending pot fragments and musket balls flying at high speed in all directions, in the same manner as a modern grenade. In the dark before dawn on September 20, 1601, when the army heard the Islamic call to prayers, they catapulted these antipersonnel bombs, or grenades, over the city walls.

Many Turks died from the explosions. Outside the city's east gate, the Christians lit fires to draw the Turks out. Duke Mercoeur used his cannons to batter the Turks while a second force led an attack across the muddy lake adjacent to the city. The Turks had not defended that flank, thinking the lake was impassable. However, the Christian warriors made a kind of snowshoe out of branches and marsh grass to keep their feet from sinking into the mud.

Caught in the cross fire, the Turks retreated into the city. The cannonade continued and eventually penetrated the city's defensive walls. Duke Mercoeur's army poured in through the breach and slaughtered every Turk who resisted. The pasha (governor of the city) retreated to the palace with five hundred of his men

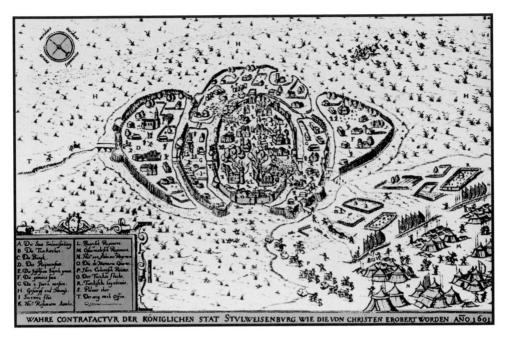

The siege at Alba Regalis, with the Duke of Mercoeur's army shown camped in the bottom right. (Ortelius Redivivus)

to make a last stand. Meldritch's men, including John Smith and his soldiers, decimated these remaining Turks and took the pasha prisoner.

Duke Mercoeur relished this particular victory. Alba Regalis had a special significance for the Hungarians, being the traditional seat of their kingdom. Duke Mercoeur's conquest of the city restored it to Hungarian control and ended fifty-eight years of Turkish occupation.

When the great Turk and Ottoman sultan Mehmet III learned of the siege of Alba Regalis, he raised an army of 60,000. The Turks marched west toward the city. Duke

45

Mercoeur thought that this newly assembled force would be inexperienced and easily repulsed. He soon learned he was wrong. Twenty thousand Christian soldiers marched against the Turks. Smith rode with his company of cavalry as part of Meldritch's regiment.

The opposing armies met at Charka Bogazi (Skirmish Gorge), about ten miles from Alba Regalis, and a bloody battle ensued. Wave after wave of attacks took place until night fell. Meldritch and his regiment were surrounded and thought they were destined to die or become Turkish prisoners, but other troops breached the Turkish line, providing an escape route for Meldritch's men.

During this skirmish, Smith had his horse killed under him, and he was badly wounded. But the indomitable captain grabbed another horse, swung up into the saddle and continued to lead his men, fighting off the Turks and returning to the Christian line. Smith wrote of the Earl of Meldritch's bravery in glowing prose, but he limited his description of his own exploits to the simple statement that he lost his horse, found another, and made it back to his regiment.

Smith said Meldritch "made his valor shine more bright than his armor, which seemed painted with Turkish blood. He slew the brave Sanzach Bugola [a cavalry officer]." When Smith and Meldritch returned to the Christian line, half of their regiment lay dead on the field of battle. Smith wrote, "It was a terror to see how horse and man lay sprawling and tumbling, some one way, some another on the ground."

The Turks, sensing a possible victory over Duke Mercoeur's army, sent 20,000 additional men to lay siege to Alba Regalis. The Turkish forces dug entrenchments on the plain outside the city to prevent the duke from returning to the city to reinforce the garrison. For several days, the opposing armies taunted each other to take the field. Finally, the duke sent forth his army. They fought fiercely. Under this intense assault, the Turks abandoned their siege on the city and retreated to camp. The Christians took two hundred prisoners and captured nine cannons. However, seeing another Turkish army entering the valley, Duke Mercoeur called his army back to the Christian encampment.

Nine or ten days passed without battle while both sides took time to replenish their supplies. The onset of severe cold weather decided the outcome. The Turks withdrew to a position on the Danube River south of Budapest, and Alba Regalis remained under control of the Christian garrison.

Duke Mercoeur learned that Archduke Ferdinand had besieged the city of Nagykanizsa, well to the southwest of Mercoeur's current position. Nagykanizsa was another important Turkish stronghold in Hungary. Mercoeur divided his army into three parts. He sent Earl Russworm with 7,000 men to assist Archduke Ferdinand at Nagykanizsa. Meldritch, along with John Smith's cavalry and an army of 6,000 men, had orders to assist Giorgio Basta in his Transylvanian campaign. The remainder of the army accompanied Duke Mercoeur to reinforce the Christian garrisons in the north Danube River valley.

In two major battles, Smith's cunning intellect and knowledge of warfare proved to be decisive in victory for the emperor's army. John Smith was no longer just a farm boy from Lincolnshire, England. He had become a battle-tested, hardened soldier.

four

BATTLE WORN, BATTLE READY

Smith, with the Earl of Meldritch's army, endured severe winter weather on the march to Transylvania (now Romania), Meldritch's homeland. Politics in Transylvania and neighboring Walachia were a muddle. John Smith was caught up in an embroiled conflict that he might not have fully understood.

At that time, three factions were in a struggle to control Transylvania: the Holy Roman Empire, led by Emperor Rudolph II and Pope Clement VIII, and in battle by Giorgio Basta, intended to restore Roman Catholicism to Hungary and Transylvania; Prince Zsigmond Báthory, the native son of Transylvania, wanted to unify the region and establish autonomous control; and the Turks, behind their puppet princes, also laid claim to the region. All three contended for ultimate control over the country.

Meldritch decided to join forces with Prince Zsigmond instead of Basta.

Smith believed, based on Meldritch's explanation, that most Transylvanians supported Prince Zsigmond. However, this struggle involved more than just political control of the region.

Prince Zsigmond opposed Turkish rule of his homeland and needed the emperor's support to regain control; but he sided with the Protestants in their religious conflict with the Holy Roman Empire. Meldritch probably had the same concerns, but his first loyalty clearly went to Prince Zsigmond. Smith believed the prince's position was the right one to support. He had confidence in the Earl of Meldritch—a veteran of twenty years of service in the emperor's army. Religion may also have influenced Smith's decision—he was, after all, a member of the Anglican Church, and his firsthand experience with the Roman Catholic pilgrims would not have encouraged him to side with the Catholics in this regional conflict.

ERZSÉBET BÁTHORY

Prince Zsigmond Báthory came from an interesting family of Transylvanians. His family tree included the infamous Vlad Dracul—also known as Vlad Tepes and Vlad the Impaler. The prince married a first cousin of Emperor Rudolph II, and the king of Poland was his uncle. But none claimed the lasting fame of Zsigmond's first cousin.

Erzsébet Báthory has been known through history as a notorious female "vampire" and the model for a number of horror movie characters.

Erzsébet Báthory.

In particular, she may have served as an inspiration for Bram Stoker's story about Count Dracula. Beset by mental illness, Erzsébet attempted to retain her youthful appearance by killing hundreds of young virgins. She bathed in the blood of her victims, convinced that it would prevent the effects of aging on her beauty. According to the legend, this incredible behavior stemmed from a day when she struck a young servant girls so hard that the girl bled. Erzsébet thought her own skin looked younger and whiter after the servant's blood was washed off. Another legend states that Erzsébet, while out riding one day, insulted an old woman, who warned her, "You laugh at me, young woman, but one day you'll be old and ugly just like me!" This event precipitated an obsessive fear of getting old.

Erzsébet was born in 1560, engaged at age eleven to Ferencz Nadasdi, and married to him by age fourteen. Her husband died in 1604, and Erzsébet progressed from being an evil mistress of her servants to a horrific predator. Over a period of six years, with the aid of several trusted servants, she lured 650 young virgins to their death by the most sadistic means. She and her accomplices finally became so careless that they threw several bodies over the wall of Castle Cachtice, where the villagers found them. Her accomplices were tried for the murders in January 1611. One damning piece of evidence in the trial was Erzsébet's diary, which carefully recorded the atrocities. Erzsébet did not stand trial due to the influence of the Báthory family. However, she did not escape punishment. The family walled her into a small room in the castle with only a small opening for food to be passed to her. She made her will on July 31, 1614, and was dead by August of that year. Her story lives on in perpetuity as books and movies find new ways to tell it.

An anonymous 1665 engraving of Zsigmond Báthory, the prince of Transylvania. (Ortelius Redivivus)

Meldritch planned to attack and regain control of the region held by the Turks. Prince Zsigmond made him camp master of his army, providing full support for his campaign. The prince also gave Meldritch's troops permission to claim all the booty they could wrest from the Turks—a powerful incentive to the soldiers.

The earl had much experience in the territory held by the Turks called the Land of Zarand. That area, surrounded by mountains, was full of Turks, Tatars, bandits, and renegades. Within those mountains lay an area Smith called the "Plain of Regall." Regall was a fortified city (now lost to history) that was considered impregnable due to its location within the mountains. The city had withstood numerous invasions and had never been taken until the Turks gained control.

During the winter, Meldritch reconnoitered the area and determined the best passage through the mountains to the city. When spring arrived, Meldritch marched his army into the area. He dispatched Colonel Veltus with his regiment to set up an ambush in a valley defended by a Turkish fort. Once the ambush was in place, Meldritch had troops round up all the local cattle and drive them along the valley. The Turks at the fort took the bait and were captured by Colonel Veltus' men when they attempted to reclaim the cattle. This action secured the passage through the valley for Meldritch's army.

The earl used the next six days to haul his heavy cannons up the muddy valley. That delay allowed the Turks to call up reinforcements. Meldritch had 8,000 men poised to attack the city when the Turks stormed out and began their own offensive. Smith wrote that a bloody battle ensued, with each side losing 1,500 men. The

Turks retreated into the city under the cover of heavy cannon fire from the ramparts.

The next day, General Moses Szekely brought 9,000 foot soldiers along with twenty-six cannons to assist Meldritch. General Szekely had captured important strongholds and had expelled the Jesuits from those areas, restoring the Protestant religion to parts of Transylvania. Thus, he did not just happen to be in the area; he clearly knew of Prince Zsigmond's aims and readily joined forces with Meldritch.

At the Plain of Regall, the Turks looked down disdainfully on the Christian army from the safety of the high city walls. They believed their well-fortified city, defended in the rear by an impassable mountain, could easily withstand the besieging army.

In spring 1602, the Christians spent nearly one month digging entrenchments and raising firing platforms for their cannon. During that time, the Turks, according to Smith, grew fat from their lack of exercise. They taunted the Christians and, "to delight the ladies," challenged the Christians to a contest of single combat. The Turks said they would send their best warrior to the field to fight the best Christian soldier. The Christians took the challenge and drew lots to select their champion. Captain John Smith won the honor.

During the contest, the Christians and Turks agreed to a truce. Ladies and men-at-arms crowded the city ramparts to watch the contest, expecting their Turk *bashi* (captain) to quickly dispatch the Christian champion.

They had not counted on Captain John Smith.

The Turk bashi was resplendent in his armor. He rode onto the field preceded by his squire, carrying a lance and wearing expensive armor decorated with silver eagle's wings on the shoulders and adorned with gold and precious gems. Smith, on the other hand, wore a mismatched collection of whatever armor the Christians had at hand.

Smith rode onto the field of combat amid a blare of trumpets, also preceded by a page carrying his lance. His extensive practice at jousting in the Lincolnshire woods and Signore Paleologue's training in horsemanship would soon be put to the test.

The two champions rode to opposite ends of the field, turned, and lowering their visors, waited for the signal to begin. At the signal, Smith spurred his horse and charged. Closing on his opponent at a gallop, Smith took deadly aim with his lance, and at the moment of collision, the point of his lance pierced the Turk bashi's visor, killing him instantly. The Turk toppled off of his horse and clattered to the ground.

Smith jumped from his horse, removed the bashi's helmet, and with his battle-axe chopped off the Turk's head and held it triumphantly aloft. The stunned Turks ran onto the field and carried their champion's headless body back within the city walls. Smith mounted his horse, rode over to the cheering Christian line, and presented the Turk's head to General Szekely. The Christian army celebrated their English champion.

The Turks were in an uproar as the Christians cheered. A friend of the slain Turk, one Smith called "Grualgo," challenged Smith to a rematch. Flushed with his victory, Smith accepted. Grualgo swore he would regain his friend's head or lose his own in the attempt. This was now a blood feud. They arranged to meet on the field the next day.

At the appointed hour, Grualgo, hot with rage, faced Smith from the opposite end of the field. When they heard the signal, both men charged across the field with their lances lowered. They crashed past each other, shattering both lances, but each man remained astride his horse. They threw down the stubs of their lances, reined in their horses, turned and fired their pistols. Smith was hit, but the ball only dented his armor. However, Smith's shot wounded Grualgo in his left arm, making him lose control of his horse.

Grualgo fell to the ground, badly injured. Smith dismounted and easily dispatched Grualgo. As Grualgo predicted, there were but two possible outcomes for this contest. Unfortunately for him, it was his own severed head that Smith carried from the field of battle, once again presenting it to the cheering Christian army.

In the ensuing days, the truce broke, and the Turks left the city to fight. The skirmishes were indecisive, but the Christians desperately needed more time to finish their fortifications. So John Smith proposed a way to hold the Turks at bay and buy some time.

Smith sent a challenge addressed to the noblewomen

of Regall. He said that he had tired of fighting "servants," but if a man of their aristocratic rank had the courage to come forward, he would fight for his head in single combat. The Turks must have been enraged by this affront to their honor. One whom Smith called "Bonny Mulgro" took up the challenge.

The next day, both warriors entered the field as before but without lances. First, they fired their pistols at each other. Neither man was harmed. They closed on

This colorized scene of Smith (right) *defeating Mulgro is from an engraving in Smith's 1630 book,* True Travels. (Courtesy of the North Wind Picture Archive.)

How he flew BONNY MVLGRO Chap. 7.

each other and, still astride their horses, hacked away with battle-axes. One of the Turk's blows sent Smith's battle-axe flying from his hand, and Smith nearly fell from his horse. The Turks on the ramparts cheered on Mulgro, sensing a quick victory. The Christians watched nervously from their ranks, shouting encouragement to the Englishman.

Despite Mulgro's advantage of the battle-axe, Smith's Lincolnshire training and experience, plus his nimble mount, gave him the edge. He avoided most of the Turk's blows and waited for his chance. As Mulgro swung his battle-axe, Smith noticed an opening below his breast-plate. Timing his move, Smith thrust his sword, stabbing Mulgro through the gap in his armor.

Mulgro plunged from his horse, mortally wounded. The Turks on the ramparts wailed in disbelief at the defeat of their third champion, while a loud cheer erupted among the Christian soldiers. Like his two predecessors, Mulgro lost his head to the young English captain.

John Smith received quite a celebration for his defeats of the three Turks. Three men, carrying the slain Turk's heads on lances and walking beside three rider-less horses, led a parade of 6,000 men. General Moses Szekely embraced Smith and gave him a splendid horse, a scimitar, and a sword-belt—worth three hundred ducats. That was equivalent to 150£ sterling in 1602 and about $34,000 today. The Earl of Meldritch made Captain John Smith the sergeant major of his entire regiment.

His studies of military history and technology, and

his practical training during his hermitage in Lincolnshire, had brought Smith this achievement. He was truly a hero of the Christian army. However, Smith's ability to endure and triumph had many more tests ahead.

Smith's three duels with the Turks bought the Christian army enough time to prepare for the attack of Regall. They now had twenty-six cannons on platforms about fifty feet high, which fired at the city walls and gates with devastating effect. After fifteen days, they breached the walls in two places. The Turks fought tenaciously even though their pasha had retreated to his castle on top of the mountain, from where he looked down on the turmoil.

General Szekely led the final assault up the steep slope to the city. Two regiments lost nearly half of their men under a hail of logs and other missiles thrown from the ramparts. They pushed on and stormed through the jagged breaches in the city walls, where they fought hand-to-hand with the city's defenders.

A second wave led by Meldritch's regiment reinforced the first attackers. Smith fought with pistol and sword in the city streets, helping to force the Turks back to the castle. With their backs to the castle walls and faced by the superior fighting force, the Turks raised a flag of truce.

However, Meldritch, the native son, remembering his father's death at the hands of other Turks, pressed on in battle. He redirected the Turks' cannons on the castle and blasted it for the rest of the day. The following day, the castle walls failed under the barrage, and the Christian army

An engraving from Smith's True Travels *depicting his version of the siege at Regall.*

streamed in, killing anyone capable of bearing arms. The Christians displayed the heads of slain Turks on stakes around the castle walls, in the same way the Turks had treated the Christians from whom they had taken the castle years before.

General Szekely had the city walls repaired and removed the siege equipment from the plain outside the walls so that it could not be used later by other invaders. As promised, the soldiers were allowed to pillage the city. Smith said that the plunder comprised a rich treasure, since the city had been the stronghold of thieves for so many years. He did not report what, if any, share of the loot he received.

Szekely lost many men in the siege of Regall. He vented his anger by commanding his army to sack three towns along the Mures River. Finally, he marched farther east along the river into Alba Iulia with 2,000 prisoners—mostly women and children.

The Transylvanian princes had their residences in Alba Iulia, and Prince Zsigmond was there in early April 1602 when John Smith, the Earl of Meldritch, and General Szekely marched triumphantly into the city. Prince Zsigmond heard the story of Smith's valor in battle and his clever strategies at Olumpagh, Alba Regalis, and Regall. In recognition, the prince promised Smith an annual pension of three hundred ducats and the right to a coat of arms bearing three Turks' heads. Smith proudly displayed the coat of arms for the rest of his life. The humble farmer's son from Lincolnshire now had the military rank and trappings of a medieval knight—at least in the Transylvanian army.

While Smith received his honors in Alba Iulia, Emperor Rudolph sent Giorgio Basta to claim Transylvania for the empire. Rudolph recognized that his control over Transylvania had been weakened by Prince Zsigmond's popularity with the Transylvanians and his recent military victories. Transylvania had at one time been a strong and productive European country, but interminable wars had left it in desolation. Weeds choked the fields. Churches, palaces, and other buildings were abandoned and covered in ivy. Peasants and merchants suffered the most, though soldiers endured broken limbs and wounds, endless marches, bad lodging, and poor diet.

Learning of the coming of Emperor Rudolph's army under Basta, and assessing his own position—he could not effectively fight the Holy Roman Empire and the Turks—Prince Zsigmond sent word to Basta that a truce be put in effect until Zsigmond's envoys could smooth out his relationship with the emperor. Basta agreed to the truce. And Zsigmond's envoys convinced Emperor Rudolph to honor a previous agreement that granted Prince Zsigmond the land of Silesia plus 60,000 ducats ($6.8 million today) immediately, with a 50,000 ducat ($5.7 million) pension thereafter.

When General Szekely learned that Zsigmond had abandoned his campaign and capitulated to the emperor, he and his men refused to be subject to "German," or Roman Catholic, rule. While John Smith and the remnants of the army from Hungary remained loyal to the prince and the emperor, General Szekely and his force attacked Basta's army and fought for about seven hours. About 6,000 men died in that intense battle. In defeat, Szekely disbanded his force and fled to join the Turks in Timisoara to the south. Since he opposed their common enemy, the Holy Roman emperor, the Turks willingly took Szekely in. Thus was the tangled political landscape of Transylvania in the early seventeenth century.

Holy Roman Emperor Rudolph II was one of the most eccentric rulers in European history. He was deeply interested in astrology, alchemy, and the occult, as well as collecting dwarves and organizing a division of giants in his army. (Kunsthistorisches Museum, Vienna, Austria)

Tranquility and stability were still a long way off in this volatile land. Smith saw much more fighting and bloodshed, and it seemed there were always at least two military forces ready to face off, with the prize being an advantage in controlling this portion

The dotted line from modern-day Hungary into modern-day Romania marks John Smith's travels during his service in the Earl of Meldritch's army.

of Europe. The Tatars, Turkic speakers and Muslims descended from the Mongolian empire and living in Russia, joined the mix, creating an added layer of complexity. The fighting culminated in a battle royal, with the Christian army at a decided numerical disadvantage. Meldritch and Smith brought 11,000 men into the valley of Veresthorn, along the Altus River at Turnu Rosu Pass. The Tatars joined the Turks in a force numbering 40,000. What was left in the end was a wasteland of mutilation and death. Smith estimated the death toll at 30,000.

John Smith was wounded in the battle, taken prisoner instead of being killed, and nursed back to health. He did not describe how badly he was wounded or how long his period of recovery lasted. He may have hoped for merciful treatment and a chance to return to England, but that was not to be. Once his captors determined he had sufficiently healed, they marched him south through Transylvania to the Danube River. Their destination was the great slave market at Axopolis near the Black Sea.

Slavery was quite common at this time in many parts of the world. Slaves of many vanquished nations, including European as well as African countries, toiled for the Turks. Slave ownership existed in many African nations, as well. Thus, John Smith's fate was not in any way unique. In fact, he would have anticipated that fate once he found himself a prisoner. His only other hope would be that his captors might attempt to obtain a ransom for him rather than sell him as a slave. Instead, Smith took his place in the slave pen and soon was sold to Pasha Bogall.

Bogall took Smith into custody and forced him to join a convoy of slaves ready for delivery to their new masters. Smith marched to Constantinople (now Istanbul, Turkey) chained by the neck, one of twenty slaves in a line. They walked about six hundred miles—an incredibly long journey lasting weeks. Although Smith could not have known it at the time, Queen Elizabeth I of England died in March of 1603, a world away from his march to Constantinople.

The slaves must have been a ragged bunch of prisoners when they finally arrived at Constantinople, where Smith met his new owner, Pasha Bogall's fiancée, Charatza Trabigzanda.

five
LIFE IN
CAPTIVITY

John Smith functioned remarkably well in every foreign society he encountered. His formal studies in England probably did not include foreign languages, but his Latin studies helped. He must have picked up some French expressions in his early travels, and perhaps he learned some Italian in addition to horsemanship from Signore Paleologue. How he managed to converse with people such as the Earl of Meldritch, a Transylvanian, is anybody's guess, but considering the many European nationalities that constituted Emperor Rudolph's army, translation from one language to another must have been readily available.

Smith called his new owner Charatza Trabigzanda, though we know now that was not her real name. That phrase is a Greek dialect meaning "Girl from Trabzon."

The city of Constantinople fell to the Ottoman Empire on May 29, 1453.
(Bibliothèque Nationale, Paris)

Trabzon is an area in Turkey on the southern coast of the Black Sea. Smith must have asked who his owner was, and they said Charatza Trabigzanda, "A girl from Trabzon." Smith, not speaking the language, assumed that was her name.

Smith described Charatza as a "noble gentlewoman." She was proud of her new slave, whom she described as a Bohemian lord, because that is what her fiancé, Bogall, told her he was. He also told her that he had conquered Smith in battle, not that he had purchased him. Bogall claimed he had conquered many other slaves in battle, and their ransom would "adorn her with the glory of his conquests."

When Smith learned Charatza spoke some Italian, he talked with her in that language as best he could, giving himself the opportunity to learn how Bogall had deceived her. Smith told her that Bogall's tale was not true. He told her how Bogall had bought him at the slave market, and he also confessed that he was an ordinary Englishman who had risen to the rank of captain through his military exploits—not a noble Bohemian lord.

Now that she knew Smith's real history, Charatza took pity on him, and apparently her pity soon changed to admiration, perhaps even infatuation. She no longer treated Smith as a slave. But Charatza and Smith had to be careful. They could not let anyone observe them acting as anything other than a noblewoman and her slave. Charatza knew that if her mother suspected how she felt about Smith, her mother would sell him to someone else to get him away from her. So Charatza devised a way to protect Smith until she was old enough to have him safely for herself.

Charatza sent Smith to her brother, who ran an agricultural station, or *timar,* in a place Smith called "Nalbrits," a town in a region of Tartaria he called "Cambia." This area has never been precisely identified, but it must have been in what is now the Rostov region of Russia.

Smith's guarded journey to Nalbrits took him from Istanbul through eastern Turkey to Varna (in Bulgaria), an ancient Black Sea port. At Varna, Smith boarded a Turkish ship and sailed east across the Black Sea, probably following the northern coast past Odessa (in the Ukraine) and the mouth of the Dnieper River, past the Crimean peninsula and through the narrow straits by Kerch that lead into the Sea of Azov.

The Turks continued across the Sea of Azov and entered what Smith said they called the "Bruapo River"— most likely the Manych River, which enters the Sea of Azov in the vicinity of the better known Don River delta. The Turkish ship took more than a week to proceed upriver to their destination. Charatza's brother lived in a "vast stony castle." The Turkish army had quarters behind the high stone walls, and Smith wrote that the local population was subjugated by the "tyrannical" Turks.

Smith expected to be treated well by Charatza's brother, the pasha of Nalbrits, whom Smith called Tymor Bashaw. Smith believed she had sent him to her brother to be

The dotted line marks Smith's journey in captivity from Istanbul (Constantinople) to Nalbrits, where he was enslaved to Tymor Bashaw.

protected for her sake, and to teach him the Turkish language and customs "till time made her master of herself," which would come with age.

Whatever Charatza or Smith expected, Tymor Bashaw's treatment of Smith was quite the opposite. He stripped Smith naked, had his head and beard shaved, and riveted an iron ring around his neck. Then he dressed Smith in a rough woolen coat.

Smith became one of nearly one hundred slaves managed by the pasha. Most were Turks and Moors, some Christians. Since Smith was the most recent arrival, his status was lowest among all slaves, who performed hard labor and existed on the most meager food. Smith said a dog could hardly have endured the treatment he received.

Tymor Bashaw and his friends dined in high style. Smith said they ate pilaf, which is boiled rice, with pieces of mutton, horse, bull, or other animals. They also ate "samboyses and muselbits," which he said were kinds of pies filled with all sorts of chopped meats and herbs. Their favorite drink was coffee made from a grain Smith called "coava." Another favorite drink was a mixture of honey, water, and mare's milk.

By contrast, Smith and the other slaves dined on horse entrails cut into pieces and boiled in a large cauldron with couscous. There was a pecking order among the slaves. Turks and Moors dined first, and the Christian slaves got what was left. The slaves ate their foul gruel from a large bowl with their dirty fingers. To supplement this diet, the slaves took some of the cooking liquid, mixed it with more couscous, and made flat bread by baking it in the coals of their fire. This bread, plus whatever scraps of meat or broth they could scrounge, sustained them.

The wealthy natives dressed like the Turks, but the rest wore sheepskins. One sheepskin served as a coat covering the upper body—two legs tied around the neck and the other two tied around the waist. A second sheepskin worn as a sort of diaper completed their suit of clothes. They wore black felt caps, and their carpets and bedding were also made from felt.

Smith believed his only hope to be released from slavery was Charatza's love. He imagined that she did not know how badly her brother was treating him. Some historians believe that Smith was being initiated into Turkish life. If so, according to Smith's description of his treatment, he suffered an extreme form of hazing. Given that Tymor Bashaw made no attempt to teach him the Turkish language, Smith's interpretation is most likely correct, and Charatza's brother probably had no intention of honoring his sister's wishes.

Smith discussed escape plans with other Christian slaves who had been there much longer. They had found escape impossible. At this point, Smith seemed resigned to live the life of a slave until a reasonable opportunity to escape presented itself. He observed, "God . . . helps his servants when they least think of help." Although, in Smith's case, "God helps those who help themselves" might have been a more apt expression.

Smith's captor had decided that he could trust him to work as a thresher in the grain fields a few miles from his home. Charatza's brother regularly inspected the work in the fields, and on those occasions he took every opportunity to beat and verbally abuse Smith. One day, Smith had had enough. He turned on Charatza's brother and struck him with his threshing bat. Smith said he

In this engraving from Smith's book True Travels, *Smith beats and kills his master, Tymor Bashaw, in order to escape from slavery.*

struck the man repeatedly in the head and "beat his brains out." Realizing the gravity of what he had done, Smith stole the dead man's clothes and horse, and hid the body under a pile of straw.

Dressed in the stolen clothes, Smith filled a knapsack with grain, mounted the horse, and rode quickly into the desert. His route took him away from the Manych River valley and into the Circassi Desert on a northeasterly course parallel to the Don River. When his excitement over his escape subsided, he awoke to the terrible realization that he had no idea where he was or where he could find a friendly reception. This unknown

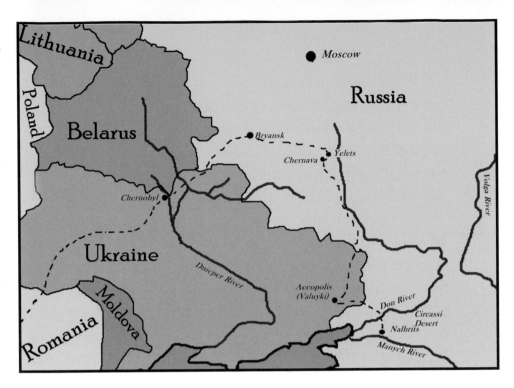

After his escape from Nalbrits, Smith trekked his way back toward Transylvania. His path is marked by the dotted lines.

wilderness presented Smith with his greatest survival challenge so far. He had endured a dunking in the Mediterranean by the pilgrims, battle at sea with Captain La Roche, and much combat on land. But in all those situations, he was among people he knew and with whom he could communicate. Now he was more alone than he had ever been, unarmed, and with no idea where he was or which way to travel to get help.

Smith rode aimlessly for a few days, never meeting another person, but then he found a marked trail. He believed God had guided him to this path, which he eventually learned was a caravan road that crossed the desert to Astrakhan on the Caspian Sea. Curious signposts marked the route for travelers and trade caravans, and the way toward the land of the Crym Tatars (west) was marked by a half moon. A rendering of a black man marked the direction to Georgia and Iran (south); a picture of the sun indicated the way to China (east); the way to Moscow (north) was indicated by a cross.

Smith put his faith in God and followed the sign of the cross. He rode for sixteen more days, probably covering about 250 miles. This journey brought him to the area of the portage between the Don and Volga rivers—an important trade route. There he found sanctuary in a town controlled by a garrison of troops from Moscow. This town stood behind a defensive wall of earth and stone, further defended by a moat and palisade.

The governor of the garrison took pity on Smith, recognizing him as an escaped Christian captive of the Turks—enemies of the Russians—and removing the iron collar from his neck. Smith received new clothing, food, and a much needed rest. There he also made the acquaintance of another important woman in his life. Like Charatza, this "good lady" that Smith called Callamata "largely supplied all his wants." Smith did not elaborate on what he meant by that enigmatic phrase.

Smith left the town with a convoy headed to Chernava in Russia. From Chernava, he traveled to the Russian Kaluga region south of Moscow. He continued westward to the region of Severski. Crossing the Dnieper River near present-day Chernobyl, Smith followed other rivers west through the Ukraine entering the eastern slope of the Carpathian Mountains at Drogobyck. Crossing the mountains, Smith headed to Sibiu in Transylvania, where he hoped to find Prince Zsigmond and the Earl of Meldritch.

Smith had an enjoyable passage through Russia and the Ukraine. He said he seldom received better respect or entertainment in his life. Although the countries had been pillaged in numerous wars, the convoys Smith traveled with were safe and well received at each stop on the long journey. The villages had few houses, and those were mere log huts with board roofs. Most villages had no significant defenses other than a ditch and palisade. Some had a few cannons as well as slings, small firearms, and muskets, though their predominant weapon was the bow and arrow.

Smith found many old friends in Transylvania, and he lingered awhile, enjoying their company. But he was anxious to rejoin Prince Zsigmond and Meldritch, who had

The beautiful Bohemian city of Prague, as drawn in the 1572 atlas, Civitates Orbis Terrarum, *edited by Georg Braun and engraved primarily by Franz Hogenberg.*

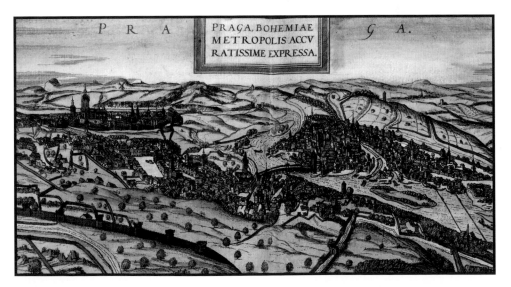

gone to Prague in Bohemia (now the Czech Republic).

At Prague, he was told that the prince had gone to Leipzig, Germany, so he continued on to that location, where they finally met. The prince and the earl were delighted to see the young captain, who they thought had died on the battlefield at Turnu Rosu. Smith had much to tell them concerning the twelve months or so they had been apart.

In appreciation for Smith's loyalty and the hardships he had endured, Prince Zsigmond presented Smith with a written grant of arms, formalizing the verbal grant he had given him more than a year before at Alba Iulia. The prince also presented him with an award of 1,500 gold ducats (worth about 750£ sterling then and about $172,000 today).

Smith remained in Germany for some time, visiting various cities before passing into France. He sailed down the Loire River and then traveled to Nantes in Brittany, where he embarked for Bilbao, finally crossing the Bay of Biscay and landing in Spain.

Smith headed to North Africa, specifically Morocco, to see if there would be an opportunity for a soldier of fortune there. For reasons unknown—curiosity per-haps—he went through Spain, which was certainly not without risk. Spain and England were not on good terms and hostile toward each other's citizens.

How Smith could travel safely with the small fortune the prince had given him is a puzzle no one has solved. Since he did not mention any difficulties during his lengthy sojourn through Western Europe, one must assume no one attempted to separate him from the 1,500 gold ducats.

Smith completed his European adventures at the southern coast of Spain sometime in 1604. Since leaving England late in 1600, he had covered at least 11,000 miles, and perhaps many more. He boarded a ship in Gibraltar and sailed to Safi, Morocco.

At Safi he met a Frenchman named Merham, who was captain of a ship. The two quickly became friends, and Merham talked Smith into accompanying a group on a

The Moroccan city of Safi in the late sixteenth century, from the Civitates Orbis Terrarum.

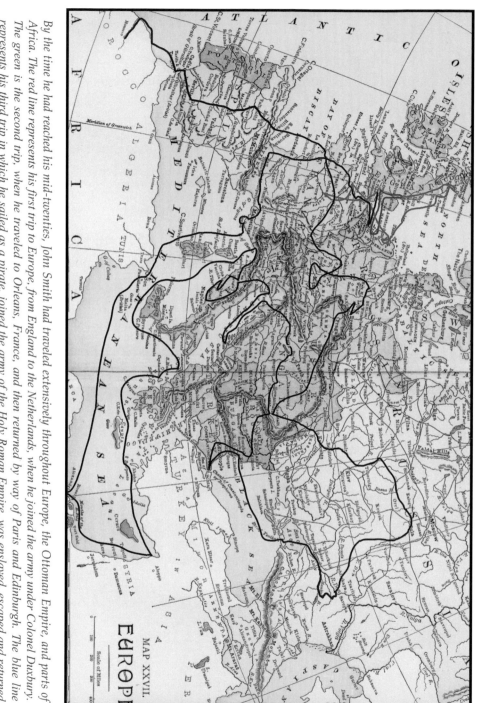

By the time he had reached his mid-twenties, John Smith had traveled extensively throughout Europe, the Ottoman Empire, and parts of Africa. The red line represents his first trip to Europe, from England to the Netherlands, when he joined the army under Colonel Duxbury. The green is the second trip, when he traveled to Orleans, France, and then returned by way of Paris and Edinburgh. The blue line represents his third trip in which he sailed as a pirate, joined the army of the Holy Roman Empire, was enslaved, escaped and returned to Europe, Africa, and finally to England.

tour of Marakesh, an ancient city noted for its monuments, situated about one hundred miles inland from the Atlantic coast. During his travels, Smith learned that the current political upheaval offered him no real possibility to sell his services as a soldier. So he returned to Safi with Merham.

Merham invited Smith and two or three others aboard his heavily armed ship, where he entertained them lavishly. What began as an unplanned excursion, when the boat rode out to sea in a terrific storm, soon turned into a privateering junket. Once the storm blew itself out, the crew spotted a bark, and they captured the vessel, which was laden with wine. They chased and overtook three or four more ships but found little except a few passengers. From them, however, they learned of five Dutch men-of-war sailing in the vicinity, so they wisely sailed away toward Cabo Bojador on the African coast.

Smith expressed no concern that Merham was a privateer—some might have said a pirate—and his journey with Merham lasted for a short while longer, enough time to engage two Spanish men-of-war in a battle that stretched over several days, filled with close encounters, hand-to-hand combat, exchange of cannon fire, and many dead. When it was over, John Smith bid Captain Merham good-bye at Safi and embarked on another ship for an apparently uneventful passage to England. Captain John Smith returned to his native land by the end of 1604. He was twenty-four.

six
THE NEW
WORLD
BECKONS

By the last quarter of the sixteenth century, England had slipped far behind a number of European countries in exploration and exploitation of the New World. A Venetian sailing under the English flag, Giovanni Caboto (also known as John Cabot) had sailed to America in 1497 and again in 1498, but following that trip England made no significant exploratory voyages until near the end of the sixteenth century. To be sure, English fishermen began to exploit the rich fishing grounds off of New England and may have had temporary encampments on shore, but concerted English efforts at exploration or settlement of the Americas lagged behind Spain, Portugal, and France.

In 1524, Giovanni da Verranzano sailed to the East Coast of North America on behalf of France. Between

1534 and 1541, Jacques Cartier, a French explorer, made three voyages to what is now Canada, exploring well into the heartland of North America. He also established a settlement in 1541, but it lasted less than one year. Samuel de Champlain, another French explorer, made several voyages to Canada, starting in 1603 and culminating with a small settlement in Quebec in 1608. He had already established a settlement in Nova Scotia (1605).

But the preeminent explorers of the Americas through all of the sixteenth century were the Spanish and the Portuguese. Columbus had sailed to America in 1492, financed by Spain. The Portuguese had sailed around

Columbus's arrival in the Bahamas in 1492, as depicted in this romanticized nineteenth-century painting, marked the beginning of a European rush to colonize the New World. (Library of Congress)

Africa and established trade outposts in India by the end of the fifteenth century. Their colonies in the West Indies, Florida, and Central and South America were well established and represented a source of huge revenues in gold as well as other commodities. King Philip of Spain seized control of the Portuguese colonies in 1580, giving Spain dominion over all the important trading centers in the Americas and also the former Portuguese outposts in India and elsewhere. England and France found themselves at a serious economic disadvantage, with so much control and wealth at Spain's disposal, and the two countries became allies in their opposition to Spain.

In 1580, Sir Francis Drake circumnavigated the globe, and by doing so he signaled England's intent to challenge Spain's dominance. Drake freely attacked and raided Spanish ships and outposts in the Americas. When he returned to England, the crown's share of the plunder he brought with him cancelled Queen Elizabeth's debts and put the country on a solid economic footing. Seven years later, Drake led a bold raid on the Spanish maritime center of Cadiz. A year from that, Spain sent its armada to attack England. Fortunately for England, the armada proved ineffective.

At about the same time, the crown had granted a patent to Sir Walter Raleigh giving him the right to explore North American territory on behalf of Queen Elizabeth I. This territory, rather vaguely described, extended from Spanish-held Florida in the south to the

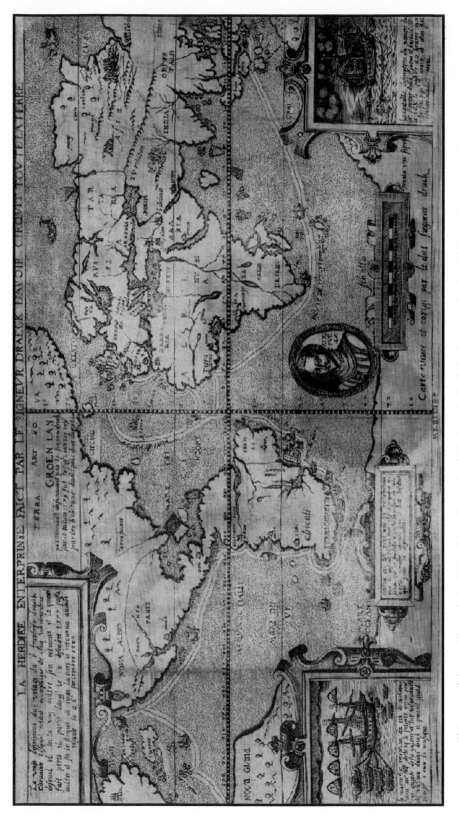

This map of the world, made in 1581, shows the route of Sir Francis Drake's circumnavigation of the earth. (Library of Congress)

Although the colonization attempt by writer and explorer Sir Walter Raleigh was ultimately unsuccessful, his experience helped pave the way for subsequent colonies to take hold.
(Library of Congress)

French-controlled territory known today as Canada. Raleigh's patent was issued on March 25, 1584. That patent empowered Raleigh to take possession of "remote heathen and barbarous lands, countries and territories not actually possessed of any Christian prince and inhabited by Christian people." Raleigh was obligated to pay the queen one-fifth of the gold and silver ore he expected to obtain in the New World.

Raleigh's expedition to the New World departed England in April 1584 aboard two ships and, after an uneventful crossing, arrived at the coast of present day North Carolina early in July. This first expedition made initial contact with the Native Americans living in the vicinity of Roanoke Island but made no attempt at colonization.

Raleigh received military advice on staging a successful colonial settlement in the territory he then called Virginia in honor of Elizabeth, the Virgin Queen. The military adviser suggested that the expedition should consist of eight hundred soldiers, some of whom would explore the interior of the country, while the remainder would build a town encircled by a fort situated on a defensible peninsula of land. The adviser further recommended that an engineer accompany the colonists to supervise the construction. Raleigh did not follow those instructions nor did later colonial expeditions. His first expedition left England with a strength of more than five hundred, but in the end only about 108 men remained behind at Roanoke Island—about half of them soldiers. Sir Francis Drake evacuated this first colony in June 1586, just four days before the relief ships arrived to replenish the colony's supplies. Fifteen men remained ashore to hold the fortified colony until another wave of colonists could arrive.

That new expedition, which would become known as the "lost colony," sailed from Plymouth on May 8, 1587, and arrived at Roanoke in July. The original plan called for them to meet with the fifteen men left behind and then continue to the Chesapeake Bay, where a more favorable site for a permanent colony was anticipated. Unaccountably, even though they found no trace of the fifteen men at Roanoke, they set up camp on the island. Eighty-five men, seventeen women, and ten boys were left at Roanoke when the fleet sailed away at the end of the summer. Those people were never seen again by the English. The resupply, scheduled for the following year, could not take place because of the Spanish Armada attack on England.

Subsequent attempts after 1590 either failed to reach Virginia or found no trace of the colonists other than a cryptic message taken to mean that some of them had gone to the village of Croatoan. As late as 1603, Raleigh dispatched Bartholomew Gilbert to look for the lost colonists in the Chesapeake Bay region. But Gilbert could not find the entrance to the bay. Instead, he went ashore near the mouth of the Delaware Bay, and Native Americans killed him. That temporarily ended attempts at locating Raleigh's colonists, but in England hope that they would be found somewhere in the Chesapeake Bay area remained.

In 1602, Bartholomew Gosnold sailed to North America with one ship and about thirty people. They explored the New England coast, visited with the Native Americans there, and scouted for suitable settlement locations. Gosnold named the most prominent site Cape Cod because of the abundant supply of fish around the settlement. Gosnold and his men remained for about one month but returned to England due to their lack of provisions.

After his adventures in Africa, John Smith returned to England in 1604 with no specific plan. He had spent all of his brief adult life as a soldier of fortune and certainly did not want to return to the rural life of

Bartholomew Gosnold is shown trading with Native Americans during his 1602 expedition in this hand-colored seventeenth-century line drawing. (Courtesy of the Granger Collection.)

Lincolnshire or the mercantile career his father had envisioned. He probably visited his mother in Lincolnshire and also ensured that the properties he had inherited were being maintained. He traveled to Ireland briefly, but the purpose of that trip is unknown. In any case, he soon made his presence felt in London. Through his influential contacts, he met several men who, impressed with his credentials, accepted him into their exciting new venture. Nothing Smith had done up to this point prepared him for the political intrigue and English class struggle in which he would become embroiled.

The key figures in this next phase of John Smith's life had some things in common with him. Captain Christopher Newport had sailed as a privateer with Sir Francis Drake, harrying Spanish shipping in the Atlantic. In 1602, while Smith fought Turks and Tatars in eastern Europe, Captain Bartholomew Gosnold sailed to New England and became even more enthused about colonizing North America. Gosnold recognized the talent in John Smith and admired his single-minded tenacity in pursuing a course of action. Gosnold was about eight years older than Smith and grew up in Suffolk, not far from Smith's home in Lincolnshire. Later, Smith would credit Gosnold with having played the leading role in planning the first successful English settlement of North America.

Gosnold was related by marriage to the Bertie brothers; he was also related to Sir Thomas Smythe, a founder of the Virginia Company. When Robert Bertie, the new Lord Willoughby, heard of Smith's exploits in Europe, Asia, and Africa, he probably recommended him to Gosnold as an experienced and resourceful person to accompany the English expedition to North America.

Walter Raleigh had assigned his rights of exploration of Virginia over to Richard Hakluyt, a geographer and writer, and to Sir Thomas Smythe, a wealthy London merchant who became one of the largest investors in the Virginia Company. Gosnold had approached these and other men with his proposal to lead an English expedition to the Chesapeake area of Virginia to plant a permanent colony as a base for exploitation of the resources of the New World. Gosnold brought John Smith into the planning process in late 1604 or by spring 1605 at the latest. Gosnold and Smith worked out the logistics of the expedition while Hakluyt, the promoter, and Smythe, the venture capitalist, worked out the organizational aspects of the Virginia Company.

Also in London at the time were five Native Americans kidnapped from northern Virginia by Captain George Weymouth in 1605. Smith and Gosnold would likely have had access to these men, as Smith seemed to have learned some of their language.

Sir Thomas Smythe, founder of the Virginia Company, had gained considerable favor and power in England in 1588 when he raised the necessary funds for Queen Elizabeth I to finance the English fleet that would destroy the Spanish Armada. (The British Library, London)

Though England and Spain had just concluded a peace treaty, international tensions still existed. The Virginia Company needed to prove that planting a colony in the Chesapeake region would not destabilize the peace. This led to an unfortunate arrangement for governance of the colony.

The Virginia Company made it clear that the colonists should do nothing to irritate the native inhabitants, whom the company sponsors expected would eagerly trade with the colonists and provide all of their food in exchange for trinkets. Therefore, the colonists did not bring the necessary tools, supplies, or skills to grow or catch their own food. They were given three priorities: find gold and silver, determine what happened to the lost Roanoke colonists, and find the mythical sea passage from the Atlantic Ocean to the Pacific Ocean.

Once the expedition reached Virginia, a seven-member board of councilors would direct the colonists. Eventually, this rule-by-committee was not suitable for what turned out to be an invasion of a foreign territory inhabited by hostile peoples. The organization forced on the colonists by the Virginia Company would quickly degenerate into bickering and outright mutiny. And Smith, used to operating under a strict, military chain-of-command, was not prepared for the politics of this new adventure.

Still, Smith invested 500£ sterling ($114,000 today) of his own funds in the enterprise. A King's Council managed the Virginia Company in London, and by November 20, the articles specifying the details of the management of the company received approval from King James . The King's Council drafted explicit written instructions that named the seven council members, specified their individual duties, and sealed those documents for the duration of the voyage to Virginia.

At that time, it was quite common for fleets to sail off on missions with sealed orders. Usually the orders were opened at sea once the fleet was isolated and the risk of enemies discovering the details of the mission were unlikely. In the case of the voyage to Virginia, the Virginia Company wanted to ensure that Spanish spies in London did not gain information that could lead them to interfere with the venture. No one among the colonists knew who the seven council members were, but most would have guessed that they would be aristocratic men of importance.

One hundred and five men departed for Virginia aboard three ships. Although Gosnold deserved the lead role because of his involvement in the entire project, Captain Newport was appointed admiral for the voyage to America. He had more experience and was twelve years older than Gosnold. Newport commanded the *Susan Constant* (120 tons), Gosnold commanded *Godspeed* (forty tons), and Ratcliffe commanded *Discovery* (twenty tons). John Smith sailed aboard Newport's ship.

The three ships weighed anchor on December 19, 1606, at Blackwell on the Thames and sailed out to sea with the tide after midnight. They sailed to the downs off

The ships that made the trip to Virginia under Captain Newport's command. From left to right: Godspeed, Susan Constant, *and* Discovery. (Library of Congress)

the coast of Kent—a staging area where ships customarily waited for favorable weather to begin their voyage. But there they had a long and uncomfortable wait. On January 30, they finally ventured far enough from land to lose sight of England. Seventeen days later, the fleet reached the Canary Islands, where they took on water and provisions for the long Atlantic crossing.

During that voyage, a dispute arose between Smith and the aristocratic passenger Edward Maria Wingfield. The two men argued, and Wingfield accused Smith of an outrageous plot of mutiny, saying that Smith planned to assassinate the trip leaders and have himself declared king when they reached Virginia. He went on to claim that Smith had confederates planted in the other ships. This fabulous allegation probably stemmed from Smith's failure to defer to Wingfield and perhaps Wingfield's own anxiety over the enterprise. In any case, Captain Newport sided temporarily with Wingfield and had Smith "restrained," or held as a prisoner.

The fleet made its next landfall at Dominica on March 24, 1607. On March 28, they landed at Nevis, where a set of gallows was erected for the purpose of hanging John Smith; however, cooler heads prevailed—probably Gosnold's intercession—and Smith was left alone, though he remained a prisoner.

The fleet spent a couple of weeks in the Caribbean foraging for supplies and, on April 21, encountered a violent storm. The storm carried them north, but they were still far enough off the coast of North America to avoid the dangerous Cape Hatteras shoals. When the weather abated, they found themselves off the Chesapeake Bay. On April 26, Newport, Wingfield, and Gosnold went ashore with about eighteen men, but Smith remained under arrest on board ship and in a bad humor.

Once again, Smith's adventurers had taken a surprising turn. Instead of leading a pioneering effort into the New World, he was bound upon an anchored ship, far away from the action.

seven

VIRGINIA'S FIRST DIPLOMAT

Their first night ashore, the expedition leaders and crew had their first encounter with Native Americans, and it did not bode well. The shore party landed near modern-day Lynnhaven Bay, Virginia, and found no sign of human habitation. They stayed ashore until night fell, and then the natives came. They charged the Englishmen and launched their flights of arrows, injuring two of the English with flesh wounds. The surprised Englishmen fired their pistols and muskets, and the attackers fled into the forest. The shore party hustled back to the ships.

That night, they read their orders and discovered who the sponsors had appointed to the council. Had the seven councilors been identified before they reached Virginia, they could have interfered with the command of the voyage and jeopardized the entire adventure before they even reached land. The seven council members were Captain Gosnold, Captain Newport, Edward Maria Wingfield, Captain John Martin, Captain George Kendall, Captain John Sicklemore (who used the alias John Ratcliffe), and Captain John Smith, the only member who could not claim to have an aristocratic heritage or a relationship to any of the major Virginia Company backers. He was a "nobody" and must have been selected for this important post by virtue of his experience as a soldier and mariner, and his demonstrated ability to rise from adversity. John Smith might have thought his vindication had come, but he would endure a few more weeks of abuse before taking his rightful place as one of the seven council members.

Over the next two weeks, the fleet explored the James River before finally settling on the tiny island they named Jamestown as their permanent base. Wingfield and Gosnold argued over the final site, but in the end Wingfield's choice won out: it afforded a more defensible, isolated position on the river; offered an unobstructed view to spot Spanish ships coming up river; and ships could sail close to shore in the relatively deep water there.

On May 14, 1607, the colonists moored their three ships close to the island where they could easily move the cargo from ship to shore and begin the task of building a defensible outpost. Smith had no say in this decision, although he later wrote that he agreed with Wingfield's choice. He continued to be treated as a

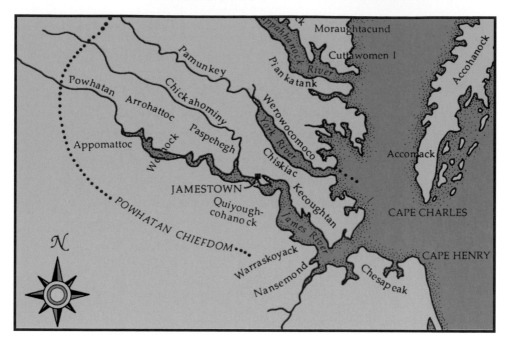

The Jamestown settlement and the surrounding areas.

prisoner in spite of the Virginia Company instructions making him a council member. His previous military experience went unheard and unheeded in the selection of the settlement location. Eventually, Smith would rise to the council position granted him—but not yet. The other council members were sworn in; Smith's enemy, Wingfield, became president of the council. Wingfield then gave "an oration" explaining to the assembled colonists that Smith had not been accepted on the council due to his alleged mutinous actions during the voyage. Of course, John Smith had not committed mutiny, but he would have to wait for an opportunity to vindicate himself.

Captain Newport put some of the colonists ashore at Jamestown to begin the building of the settlement, and he embarked on a voyage up the James River with the remainder of the colonists and ship's crew, showing the flag and attempting to make peace with the native population while looking for evidence of precious metals and a water route west to the Pacific. The focus of the expedition, as dictated by the London sponsors, was one of discovery. Newport took Smith with him, perhaps to separate him from Wingfield and avoid further conflict. At a village called Arrohattoc, Smith and Newport first heard of Powhatan, described as the overlord to whom all the tribal chiefs, or weroances as they were called, owed fealty.

Powhatan led a dominion of 14,000 Native Americans in the Tidewater area of Virginia. They spoke the language and ascribed to the culture of the Algonquins, as did many tribes along the East Coast. The approximately thirty tribes under Powhatan took their names from the rivers and streams that defined their territory, including the Paspahegh, Mattaponi, and Pamunkey. They lived in longhouses constructed from bent sapling frames covered with woven reed mats. Their diet consisted of wild peas, squash, pumpkin, and fruits and berries, with the staple being corn that they cultivated. They also ate fish and game that they hunted in the forests and grew tobacco for religious or ceremonial purposes. Their clothing came from deer skin and other animal pelts.

Powhatan ruled over a wide area bounded by the Potomac River and the Chesapeake Bay and extending south beyond James River. To the north and west, hostile tribes of the Siouan language, part of the Manahoac confederacy, were Powhatan's principal enemies.

During the voyage up the James River, Smith began to understand the Native Americans' inherent hostility toward the English. They wanted the trading opportunities but did not want the English to colonize the land.

During Newport's absence, Paspahegh Indians attacked Jamestown with a force of two hundred warriors. The colonists suffered some casualties and might have been overrun except for the ships' cannons, with which they repelled the attack. Wingfield had opposed erecting fortifications in the belief that doing so would send a hostile signal and violate the Virginia Company's instructions.

However, this second hostile attack in a matter of just a few weeks made it clear to the colonists that they should look to their own defense first and worry about the instructions later. As they cut timber and placed the logs in the soil to erect their triangular palisade (a row of pointed stakes set up as a defense), the Native Americans made several more raids but failed to inflict further injuries, except for Eustace Clovell, who was shot with a number of arrows. He died of those wounds eight days later. This crude fort resembled many of the simple defenses erected around small villages that Smith had seen in his travels through the Black Sea, Russia, and the Ukraine.

By June 6, the strain of the attacks and the labor to build the fort caused the colonists to revolt. They drew

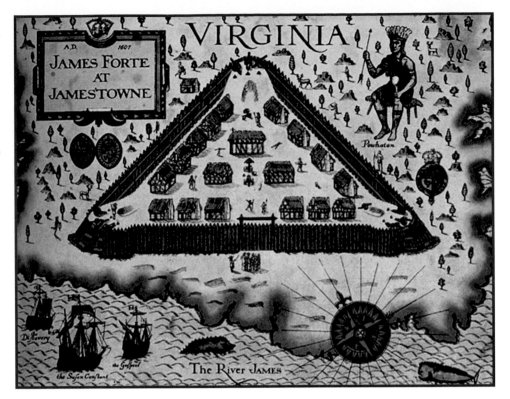

The triangle-shaped fort at Jamestown was completed only a month after the settlers' arrival at the site. (Library of Congress)

up a petition outlining their concern over Wingfield's reluctance to erect fortifications that would protect them from the natives. They also chafed at the way John Smith had been denied his rightful place on the council. Captain Newport's return four days later resolved the issue.

What was called for in this expedition was a clear line of authority. Smith could see that the insecure circumstances of the colony and the pompous, class-conscious attitude of many of the colonists cried out for strong authoritarian and competent leadership. Unfortunately, the Virginia Company had set up rule-by-committee in Jamestown. Inevitably, factionalism among the council members resulted in weak decisions and dire consequences.

Once Newport convened the council, they heard the petition and complaint, and rendered their first decision: the colonists should work together. The council also, at last, appointed John Smith to his rightful place among them. Presumably he had impressed Newport with his trustworthiness and his dedication to the assigned tasks on their trip up the James River. Finally, Smith could move freely among the colonists and apply his experience and abilities in the leadership of the Virginia expedition.

Twelve days later, Captain Newport set sail for England with a cargo of clapboards and what he thought was gold ore, leaving the now six-man council and the unsettled colonists on their own in the wilderness. He promised to return as quickly as possible with more provisions and more settlers.

A cross-section of English colonists were left at Jamestown. Captains Gosnold, Wingfield, Martin, and Ratcliffe remained, and men from the lower classes of English society also stayed behind, cutting clapboard for shipment back to England and performing the other labor that could not be avoided. President Wingfield had many problems facing him. The council was still divided, and arguments continued over the best way to safeguard the settlement.

Plus, they had few resources. Only the *Discovery* and a small sailing barge remained. Most of the weaponry that so frightened the natives sailed away on the two larger ships now headed for England. The settlement was in a precarious position during the last half of 1607. Some colonists seemed content to sit idly and wait for Newport to return with supplies and laborers, while others, John Smith among them, took a more realistic approach. Smith knew that it would be months at best before Newport could return, and winter was approaching. They had to secure adequate food and water on their own. And they also needed shelter from the winter weather.

But the knowledge that Newport had left them with what they believed were ample rations, along with the heat of the Virginia summer, led to a lazy torpor among many in Jamestown. The lack of common sense and poor discipline of his fellow colonists greatly frustrated Smith. He knew that thirteen weeks of food would never suffice—their voyage to Virginia had taken longer. They might not see Newport for six months. Perhaps he would never return; the Roanoke settlers had been victims of just that fate.

As soon as Newport's ships sailed over the horizon, the Native Americans with whom the colonists had become friendly—they had provided the colonists with advice on defending themselves against hostile tribes—began to ask awkward questions: Where had the ships gone? When would they return? Wingfield said they had sailed to Croatoan to search for the lost colonists from Roanoke. This lie would not hold up for long. Smith was concerned because he did not want the Native Americans to know they were alone.

As the days went on, the colonists began to realize that their food stocks were becoming alarmingly low. They attempted to trade with the Native Americans, who claimed they did not have any food to trade. Then, some colonists accused Wingfield of hoarding food for himself and his few loyal supporters. Also, the beer had run out and the colonists were forced to drink water—something they had little experience with (in England, water was often contaminated and dirty, making it much safer for most citizens to drink weak beer).

The inevitable happened. Beginning in August, colonists began to succumb to weakness, disease, and starvation. Each colonist received a daily ration of one cup of water-soaked barley. They slept on the damp ground without adequate shelter, and the oppressive heat, humidity, and insects took their toll. John Ashby was the first to die. Bartholomew Gosnold, the spirit of the colony, followed on August 22 after three weeks of illness. He received a hero's burial befitting the man most responsible for the expedition's planning. Archaeologists recently uncovered a grave near the west wall of the Jamestown fort, believed to be that of Bartholomew Gosnold. They found his ceremonial captain's staff of office resting at his side in the grave.

As Gosnold lay dying, Smith and Wingfield had an argument in the sick tent. Smith accused Wingfield of hoarding food. Wingfield said Smith had "begged in

Native Americans had cultivated corn as a source of food in North America for hundreds of years preceding the arrival of European settlers. Planted in spring to take advantage of the spring rains, the ears were harvested by hand in the fall to be made into grain. (Courtesy of the North Wind Photo Archive.)

Ireland like a rogue." Smith decided to openly oppose the pompous, arrogant, and ineffective president. The English class system was clearly at the base of the dispute between Wingfield and Smith. Smith felt he had earned the right to be treated as an equal. Wingfield looked down on Smith as a commoner who had insinuated his way into the expedition based on his account of his exploits in military service. Wingfield would never lower himself to take counsel from such a person.

Deaths occurred weekly during August, most from illness, but two were killed in attacks by Native Americans. Nineteen of the approximately one hundred colonists left behind by Captain Newport died in August 1607. Nearly fifty more would die before Newport's return.

Near the end of August, natives came with corn to trade. The debilitated condition of the settlement and the prospect of trade led to a political coup within the leadership of the colony. First, the council removed George Kendall from office and confined him aboard the *Discovery*. Kendall had been a consistent opponent of Wingfield and managed to interfere with every action the president and council attempted. He was confined aboard the small ship, or pinnace, to keep him out of the way and eliminate his potential influence on the other colonists. Then John Ratcliffe, John Smith, and John Martin, now a majority of the five remaining council members, moved to depose Wingfield. Wingfield joined Kendall in isolation aboard the pinnace. The council elected Ratcliffe as its new president on September 10, 1607.

On September 17, Wingfield was tried and convicted of making slanderous statements about John Smith and John Robinson—Wingfield said Smith was "intend[ing] to usurpe the government, murder the Councell, and make himself king, that his confederats were dispearsed in all the three ships, and that divers of his confederates that revealed it, would affirme it." The council ordered Wingfield to pay Smith two hundred pounds sterling.

Smith could now feel fully vindicated for the mistreatment he had suffered from Wingfield. However, Smith stayed focused on the needs of the colony and began a series of trading expeditions, sailing the barge into the Native American-controlled territories. The council appointed Smith to the position of cape merchant on September 19, putting him in charge of obtaining and dispensing the supplies of the colony.

Of course, the most needed supply was food, and Smith went in search of all he could find, making several dangerous trips up the James River and its tributaries between September and December. Toward the end of this period, only about six able-bodied men could be found at Jamestown. Some had deserted the settlement and gone to live with the natives—an indication of how desperate the conditions had become.

Smith would not live with the Native Americans for two reasons: he felt a duty as one of the leaders of the colony to build and maintain a viable settlement in Virginia, and he did not trust the Native Americans. They had taken English lives previously, and he correctly surmised that Powhatan did not want to see a permanent English presence in his land. He expected Powhatan to do all he could to cause the colony to fail. Smith brought what the tribe could spare back to the starving colonists. Each death reduced the demand for food, but seeing his fellow colonists succumb to disease and starvation drove Smith to take even greater risks.

The colonists did not respond well to unexpected conditions nor did they alter their plans and strategy for survival. They continued to underestimate the intelligence of Native Americans in matters of trade, offering little of value for the food they had harvested. Likewise, it took some time before the colonists took advantage of the local game and the fish found in the James River.

As cooler weather set in while Smith was on these trading expeditions, the colonists' tempers heated up. Captain Kendall began a campaign to persuade some of them to seize the *Discovery* and sail home to England. Compounding the problem, Ratcliffe turned out to be as bad a president as Wingfield, exhibiting the same arrogant, insolent attitude toward the colonists.

Fortunately, Smith returned in time to learn of the mutinous plans before they could be carried out. The way he discovered the plot illustrates the skullduggery at work in the colony. James Read, a blacksmith, had an argument with Ratcliffe. In the course of the conflict, Read may have started to strike the president. This was a serious offense, since the president acted as the ki=ng's agent in the colony. Read was tried, convicted, and on his way to the gallows when he told of the conspiracy to seize the pinnace and abandon the colony. He said Kendall started it and he also implicated Wingfield.

Smith arrived on the scene just in time to see the ship slipping away from its mooring. He ordered shots fired from muskets and a light cannon, and the ship moved no farther. Kendall and Wingfield ended up back in custody. Read received a stay of execution as the conspirators stood trial. Kendall confessed that he planned to steal the ship, but then he startled the jury by saying he intended to sail to Spain, where he would have provided information to King Philip about the vulnerability of the English colony. Whether Wingfield knew about Kendall's real intentions is unknown. The jury sentenced Kendall to death by firing squad, since a gentleman could not be hanged like a common criminal.

After the aborted mutiny, Smith departed on another voyage up the James River. By this time, Ratcliffe, Martin, and others had grown jealous of Smith's emerging leadership. They saw his trip to explore the Chickahominy River as an opportunity to eliminate him—perhaps permanently. This expedition would give Smith the chance to explore for the path to the Pacific Ocean that the sponsors wanted to find. According to the mythology surrounding the way to the Pacific, a river leading to a large lake would provide the access to the western ocean. Smith, with little knowledge of the Chesapeake Bay region and no idea that even larger rivers lay beyond the James River basin, thought the lake might be up the Chickahominy. If Smith could find the mythical lake, it would put him in good stead with the sponsors.

Smith sailed the barge as far up the Chickahominy as

possible—the river at that point was barely wider than the beam of the barge. Seeing they could go no farther, Smith found two Native Americans with a canoe. They agreed to take him up the river. He told them he wanted to hunt ducks, preferring not to reveal his true objective.

Leaving most of his men on the barge with orders not to go ashore, Smith and two men, Jehu Robinson and Thomas Emry, boarded the log canoe and set out upstream. They paddled about twelve miles through a maze of marshes and minor channels. Smith ordered the Native Americans to beach the canoe and cook a meal. He left Robinson and Emry behind with one native, advising them not to let down their guard and to fire a musket if they

This contemporary hand-colored wood engraving depicts Smith, wearing the red hat and cape, during one of his expeditions into the Chesapeake Bay region. (Courtesy of the North Wind Picture Archive.)

encountered or sighted any other natives. Smith, with the other Native American, proceeded on foot. Back at the barge, the situation soon deteriorated. One of the men Smith left behind, George Cassen, disobeyed orders and went ashore. He soon found himself at the mercy of natives who had been watching the barge from the forest. They tied Cassen to a tree and demanded to know where Smith had gone. Cassen refused to tell them until they began cutting off his fingers and toes. Eventually Cassen told his tormentors what he knew, but he confessed too late. They skinned him alive, set fire to the tree, and watched as the tree and Cassen burned to the ground.

Soon a large band of Native Americans set off after Smith through the dense forest. In short order, they found the canoe, and Robinson died in a hail of arrows. Emry and the other native disappeared without a trace.

Smith had not long left the two Englishmen when he heard a shout but no musket shot. Suspecting treachery, he seized his companion and tied himself to the man so that he could not escape. He threatened to shoot the hostage with his pistol if he did not cooperate.

An arrow glanced off Smith's thigh. He saw two natives approaching and he fired at them. In the time it took him to reload, several more men arrived with their bows drawn. His second pistol shot scattered them. The Native Americans fired many more arrows, and Smith fired several more volleys from his pistol—a standoff. By this time, Smith found himself surrounded by a large force; he estimated two hundred. The natives laid down their weapons, and Smith's hostage talked to them in an attempt to resolve things peacefully.

The Native Americans said that the other Englishmen were dead, but they would spare Smith, calling him the English weroance, if he would only lay down his pistol. Smith hesitated and then began to back away, pulling his companion with him. Unfortunately, he stepped into a sinkhole in the marshy ground and could not extricate himself. He was at their mercy and laid down his pistol.

True to their word, the men pulled Smith out of the freezing bog and brought him to their weroance, Opechancanough, Powhatan's half brother, who led the Pamunkey tribe. Smith and Opechancanough remembered each other from an earlier meeting at the upper reaches of the James River. Smith had a high regard for Opechancanough. He knew his life depended on convincing the weroance that he was no ordinary Englishman. He used a portable compass to impress the Native-American leader, who had never seen such a magical device. Then, Smith launched into a long-winded explanation of astronomy—the motion of the moon, sun, and planets.

After an hour of Smith's oratory, the Native Americans tired of his game and tied him to a tree. But Opechancanough had a change of heart. Smith had impressed him with his bravery in the face of overwhelming force and had dazzled him with the technology of the compass. Opechancanough decided that it might be a mistake to kill John Smith at that time.

The Pamunkeys untied Smith and, with much ceremony, they paraded him to their hunting camp. Opechancanough took the lead with a phalanx of warriors protecting his flanks and rear. Smith marched right behind him. When they entered the camp, they paraded in snakelike fashion around the clearing as the women and children watched. Then the warriors broke ranks and danced around Smith and Opechancanough in a ring.

The Native Americans took Smith under guard to a longhouse, where they served him a quarter of venison for his supper. Although he remained a prisoner, constantly guarded, he spent several otherwise pleasant days during which they continued to feed him lavishly, so much so he began to think they might be cannibals, fattening him up for the cooking pot.

During this initial captivity, the weroance of the Paspaheghs, who had attacked Jamestown, visited with Smith, and later went to Jamestown and reported that the Pamunkeys had captured him. Smith put his time in captivity to good use, learning as much as he could about the local rivers. He also learned that Englishmen—survivors from the lost colony—lived at a place called Ocanahonan.

Smith came up with a strategy to gain his release. He wrote a note to the Jamestown colonists to let them know that he was alive and well. In the note he warned them that the Native Americans planned to attack the fort again.

He gave instructions that the Native-American messengers should witness a show of force. Surprisingly, Opechancanough agreed to have runners take Smith's note to the colonists. He may have done so since it gave him the opportunity to get his spies inside the fort. When the runners arrived, the colonists adhered to the directions in Smith's message. They provided a frightening display of firearms.

When the runners returned from the fort to Opechancanough's village, they brought a letter for Smith. He read the letter aloud, and his "talking paper" mystified the natives—they knew nothing of the written word. Opechancanough decided to take the English weroance to meet Powhatan and determine what to do with him. But they took a circuitous route, marching all the way to the Rappahannock River and a village near the modern-day town of Tappahannock, Virginia. This diversion may have been taken to let the American Indians there see if Smith was the person who had kidnapped men from their tribe during an earlier voyage. Smith did not resemble that man, and eventually Opechancanough marched him back down to the York River, and in time they arrived at Werowocomoco, Powhatan's village. Held captive in a longhouse there, Smith encountered Pocahontas for the first, and most fateful, time.

Thanks to Smith's proven gift for learning foreign languages, he and Powhatan were able to talk about the English intentions (Smith used sign language to make up for gaps in the language). Smith avoided the real purpose of the English presence and talked instead of war with Spain, interest in trade, and other excuses for being there. He took the opportunity to find out what he could about the lost colony. Their

Chief Powhatan sits in state in one of the longhouses in Werowocomoco. This engraving was taken from Smith's Generall Historie of Virginia. (Library of Congress)

conversation led to no obvious conclusion, so Powhatan turned Smith over to the shamans in hope that they could use their magic to conjure up an appropriate conclusion regarding what to do with this unflappable Englishman.

In front of a fire, the shamans began a ritual that culminated with the entrance of "two sacrificial stones." The natives dragged Smith to this makeshift altar, where they placed his head. The participants appeared ready to take his life. As these events occurred, Pocahontas, at the time eleven years old, watched, horrified at the danger to the defiant Englishman. She cried out in protest before rushing to Smith's side and placed herself next to him, in the way of any blows.

It's not known what Powhatan intended for Smith. The Englishman clearly believed Powhatan had marked him for death, and he expressed great relief, both at the time and later in his writing: "In the utmost of many extremities, that blessed Pocahontas, the great King's daughter of Virginia, oft saved my life." Historians and anthropologists now know that the Native Americans incorporated much ritual and ceremony into their everyday activities and that mock execution did occur frequently. But from Smith's perspective, Pocahontas saved him from certain death.

After this event, Powhatan needed to ensure his friendship. Neither he nor Smith knew when Captain Newport might return with the heavily armed ships and reinforcements, but Powhatan knew he did not want to send an angry

The famous story in which Pocahontas begs her father to spare John Smith's life has been depicted in dozens of ways. This painting is from the nineteenth century. (Library of Congress)

John Smith back to his newly empowered settlement, which might then attack the natives' village.

In a final ceremony, during which Powhatan, painted black, made a grand entrance, the overlord informed Smith that they were friends, and he was free to return to Jamestown. Powhatan said he considered Smith his adopted son. He also made Smith the weroance of a neighboring territory and said, in return, all he wanted was a grindstone and two cannons. Smith agreed. It was the first day of January 1608.

That same day, Smith crossed the York River and made his way back towards Jamestown accompanied by a small band of Native American escorts. They brought food as presents for the colonists and expected to return to Powhatan with the cannons and grindstone. The journey took two days, the escorts insisting on stopping overnight at a campsite in the forest.

Smith received a warm welcome at the fort from nearly everyone. Only his political foes held back. Smith then presented two cannons, each weighing more than a ton. As he undoubtedly knew, the warriors, strong though they were, could not carry those cannons and a grindstone back to Werowocomoco. When Smith had one of the cannons fired as a demonstration for the warriors, they fled from the fort. After they crept back, Smith presented them with gifts for their enjoyment as well as presents for Powhatan and his extended family. But these gifts were not exactly what Powhatan was expecting. Gifts other than armaments would leave the Virginia tribal leader angry. And with a faction of enemies within the settlement, Smith felt pressure squeezing from both sides.

eight

KEEPING THE FLAME ALIVE

Though many colonists were glad to see Smith return from Werowocomoco, they were still making plans to abandon the settlement and sail the pinnace back to England. During Smith's absence, the only thing that prevented their absconding from Jamestown was the severe winter weather. Now that the weather had broken in early January 1608, John Smith stood, his feet planted firmly on the bank of the James River, opposing them.

Captain Gabriel Archer, one of the principal advocates of abandoning the settlement, plotted to dispose of John Smith once and for all. He blamed Smith for the deaths of the men who had accompanied him up the Chickahominy River. Archer said biblical law required Smith's execution—an eye for an eye. President

Ratcliffe agreed and sentenced Smith to be executed the next day.

Providentially, Captain Newport sailed up to the shore at Jamestown that very night, and Smith escaped execution for the second time in less than a week. Had Smith and his Native-American escorts not spent the preceding night in the woods, Newport would have arrived to find John Smith dead and perhaps buried along with more than half the men Newport had left months before. Newport was two months late. The "gold" ore he had returned to London proved worthless, to his embarrassment, and the resulting upheaval among the sponsors caused considerable delay in equipping the resupply fleet.

Newport quickly restored order, releasing Smith from his legal predicament, reinstalling him in good standing on the council, and announcing the appointment of Matthew Scrivener to a council seat. Scrivener was one of eighty fresh colonists brought by Newport on this first resupply trip to Virginia.

The new men, who must have appeared as saviors to the forty or so starving survivors, went right to work building new shelters. An additional forty colonists would arrive soon on a ship commanded by Captain Thomas Nelson. But fate dealt Jamestown a cruel blow when fire broke out on January 7, destroying all of the colonists' work. The fire destroyed nearly everything of value, including all but three small structures. Even the new provisions were mostly lost. Then, to make matters worse, winter weather returned with a

Christopher Newport, captain of the expedition to Virginia. (Library of Congress)

vengeance, and death followed on the heels of the cold.

Newport urged the colonists to rebuild and debriefed Smith on his explorations and his captivity. Newport would have heard from many of the unbiased colonists that John Smith had saved them during the starving times by effectively trading for food. Smith's description of Powhatan and his far-reaching authority impressed Newport. Newport's embarrassment over the worthless ore rankled, and by using Smith's connections with Powhatan, he saw an opportunity to find real gold. If gold were to be found, Powhatan would surely know where to look for it.

Smith's status with Powhatan seemed reinforced by the frequent arrival at Jamestown of gifts of food sent by the ruler, often accompanied by his daughter,

Pocahontas. The affection between Smith and Pocahontas was evident in the way they enjoyed each others' company at the fort. Smith found the energetic eleven-year-old child a cheering contrast to the morose, demoralized men who milled absently about the fort.

Newport and Smith soon found themselves in disagreement over a vital economic issue. The colonists used no judgment in bartering for food. Copper pieces were the principal currency of exchange, and Smith observed that the colonists had allowed the Native Americans to demand increasingly inflated amounts of copper for their corn. Where an ounce would have sufficed for a quantity of food a few months before, now they demanded a pound of copper. Newport failed to see this as a problem. He focused on keeping Powhatan happy at all costs so that he could learn where to find gold.

Near the end of February, with the return of milder weather, Newport and Smith, along with about forty men, set sail in the pinnace for Werowocomoco. They sailed uneventfully down the James River, up the Chesapeake Bay and the York River to Powhatan's village. As they stood offshore, they became uneasy about the reception they would get. Smith volunteered to take a party of twenty men ashore to ensure Powhatan's friendly reception before risking Newport and the others in a potentially bloody encounter. Newport readily agreed to the plan.

Smith and his men, protected in quilted leather jackets—a form of armor—proceeded to Powhatan's village unmolested by the Native Americans. Smith received a warm welcome in Powhatan's lodge and sat at a place of honor at the great chief's side. The English captain presented gifts of clothes and a white greyhound. Powhatan, through three spokesmen, gave effusive thanks for the gifts and expressions of friendship. A rich feast followed these pleasantries.

When Powhatan finally spoke, he asked Smith where the promised cannons were. Smith said he had "proffered" them, but Powhatan's men had refused. Powhatan laughed good-naturedly and said perhaps Smith could give them some lighter, more portable ordnance. Smith's men, who had remained on guard, then came in two at a time to pay their respects to Powhatan and to receive food from the great man's larder. Smith had warned the men not to let down their guard, as the villagers greatly outnumbered them.

Powhatan asked Smith to have his men lay down their arms. Smith diplomatically avoided that and said that his "father," Captain Newport, would visit with Powhatan the next day. He also said that he and Newport would vanquish Powhatan's enemies who occupied the piedmont area. Smith and Newport wanted an excuse to explore that area, where they expected gold would be found.

The great overlord reaffirmed his elevation of Smith to the status of weroance and promised that the English would have access to all the corn they needed. He also provided them food and lodging for the night in the village. The next morning, Smith, Powhatan, and their men went to the river shore in time to see Newport and a small party disembarking from one of the longboats.

With a fanfare of trumpet music, Newport strode triumphantly ashore and received a cordial greeting from Powhatan. The Englishmen and the Native Americans soon got down to business, and Powhatan proved to be a canny bargainer. He soon got the better of the newly arrived and naïve Newport. Smith watched as the cost of desperately needed food inflated before his eyes in the inexperienced negotiations led by Newport.

Smith stepped in and changed the medium of exchange to blue glass beads—a novelty Powhatan had not seen before. With this tactic, Smith drove the cost of food back down. This state visit continued for several more days, during which Newport, Smith, and Powhatan discussed various ventures. Then as a traditional sign of good faith, Captain Newport left colonist Thomas Savage as a hostage in exchange for a Native American named Namontack.

When Smith and Newport returned to Jamestown, political ferment continued among the council members. Newport, backed by a majority of the others, insisted on putting all their manpower into the quest for gold-bearing ore. The English were obsessed with finding gold and silver, as the Spanish had done so successfully. The difference was, of course, the Spanish had stolen the gold from the Native Americans who had mined and refined it. The tidewater natives had no gold or silver. While Virginia would produce some gold in time, the cursory search that Newport had made and the imprecise assaying (verifying) techniques he carried out led to failure.

Smith and Scrivener opposed searching for gold, arguing that their first priority should be efforts to ensure the survival of the colony. Smith watched with growing frustration as all efforts went into digging, assaying, and loading ore onto Newport's ship. During this protracted stay, the mariners consumed all of the provisions originally intended for the colonists. On April 10, 1608, Newport sailed back to England and his ultimate embarrassment with another cargo of useless dirt.

To Smith's great relief, Newport also had on board his England-bound ship two of Smith's biggest antagonists: Edward Maria Wingfield and Gabriel Archer, who took the chance to escape from Jamestown. Namontack, the Native-American hostage, sailed to England with Newport as well.

Now the council consisted of President Ratcliffe, Captain Martin, Matthew Scrivener, and John Smith. According to the articles, the president had two votes so that a deadlock on decisions could be avoided. Ratcliffe, never very presidential, had injured his hand in a shooting accident, and he idled away his days nursing his wound.

The future of the colony clearly rested in the hands of John Smith and Matthew Scrivener. They mobilized

The building and repair of the Jamestown settlement required the difficult tasks of clear-cutting the land and felling large trees for building material. Up to three or four men were often needed to carry each log used in the wall that surrounded the settlement. (Courtesy of the Granger Collection.)

the necessary efforts to repair the palisade walls, reroof the storehouse, and plant corn. Agriculture, up until then, had not seemed necessary to the colonists. Smith knew that they could not depend exclusively on trade or wait for resupply from England. Also, their supply of blue beads would not last much longer in the inflated market Newport had created before he left.

With the current state of friendly relations, the Native Americans were frequent visitors to the fort. Unfortunately, they did not understand the English idea of private property and some were so bold as to attempt to take things right out of the colonists' hands. Smith had to act decisively to end this aggression. With the council's approval, Smith had one of the thieves put in the stocks—he had stolen two swords. When Smith confronted another thief, the Native American started to swing his tomahawk. That man found he had made a serious mistake and ended up lying wounded at Smith's feet. Other natives rushed in to help their comrade, and Smith charged at them, brandishing his sword. He had faced much worse when he battled the Tatars in Transylvania. The Native Americans dispersed into the woods.

Over the next few days, various Native Americans came back to make their peace, returning stolen objects and offering to help the colonists with their work. Smith's strong resolve met with respect among the natives.

Unfortunately, some of Smith's fellow colonists felt his actions violated the Virginia Company instructions regarding how to deal with the native population. Once again, Smith found himself in conflict with some of the settlement when, on April 20, Captain Nelson sailed into Jamestown with forty passengers and supplies aboard the *Phoenix*. With strengthened numbers, Smith proposed a large armed expedition to carry out the exploratory duties described in the Virginia Company's instructions. Nelson would have none of it unless he and his mariners received compensation for those extra duties. The expedition did not take place, and to some colonists' chagrin, Smith remained at Jamestown, redoubling his efforts to whip the settlement into shape.

The Virginia Company seal featured King James I, who, in 1606, granted the charters for the colonization in the New World.

As if Smith's troubles were not enough, Powhatan began to apply pressure. Newport had given him twenty swords in trade for turkeys. Now Powhatan wanted more of the English weapons. Smith, of course, was not about to add to Powhatan's arsenal, knowing the arms would likely be turned on the English.

Raids by Native Americans began slowly, with the theft of an axe, and then escalated. In one encounter, Native Americans threatened Smith and Scrivener when they found them in the cornfield. The men ran into the fort and slammed the door behind them, trapping some of their pursuants inside the palisades. The council, alarmed by the aggression, voted to put ten of the Native Americans in jail.

Then Smith learned that two Englishmen, caught outside the fort, were being held hostage. He led a small party out in the barge, and they threw torches into some Native-American villages, setting fires. This brought the return of the two English hostages. Smith applied pressure to the Native Americans in the jail at Jamestown to learn what prompted their attacks. To stimulate their confessions, Smith had one of the prisoners taken into the pitch-black cargo hold of the *Phoenix*. He tied the man to the mast and surrounded him with six musket-armed men. The smoldering musket matches provided the only illumination in the inky hold. The Native American soon confessed that Powhatan and his subordinate weroances intended to disarm the English by various traps.

Powhatan's hostage, Thomas Savage, had been sent to the fort to give John Smith a present of turkeys. Smith gave Savage a message for Powhatan: the English wanted peace and would come to Werowocomoco as friends, but if they directed one arrow at an Englishman, John Smith would destroy them. Smith also instructed Savage to ask Powhatan to send a Native American named Weanock to be his guide.

Savage delivered the message to Powhatan and soon returned to Jamestown. Powhatan demanded a new hostage; apparently he feared Savage knew too much about their plans. For his part, Smith interrogated his prisoners again, and they confirmed Powhatan's intention to disarm the colonists.

Powhatan finally played his trump card. He sent Pocahontas with an escort to Jamestown to try to beguile John Smith. They brought a gift of a deer and bread, and attempted to assure Smith that Powhatan loved and respected him. They were soon joined by Opechancanough, who entreated the council to release the prisoners. The council agreed, and a temporary peace ensued.

As the final stages of loading Nelson's ship took place, Smith wrote a letter to the Virginia Company giving his report of the events that had taken place since

Smith's first published work of many appeared in England while he was still living in the New World.

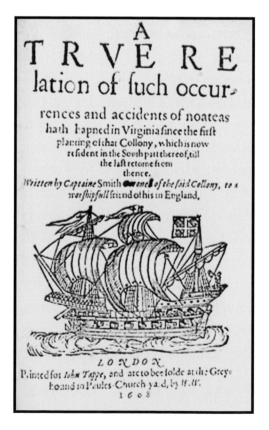

A TRVE RElation of such occurrences and accidents of noate as hath hapned in Virginia since the first planting of that Collony, which is now resident in the South part thereof, till the last returne from thence.

Written by Captaine Smith Coronell of the said Collony, to a worshipfull friend of his in England.

LONDON.
Printed for John Tappe, and are to bee solde at the Greyhound in Paules-Church yard, by W.W.
1608

sailing for Virginia. His letter, although not written for public consumption, would soon appear throughout London, published by John Healey as *A True Relation of such occurrences and accidents of note, as hath happened in Virginia*. . . Nelson sailed June 2, 1608, and an abbreviated version of Smith's lengthy letter appeared in print ten weeks later.

Smith also sent a map of the region he had explored so far, augmented with other information he had learned from the Native Americans. He still believed that a passage to the Pacific lay not far away, and he intended to explore and map that route for the sponsors.

nine

PRESIDENT AND EXPLORER

Only three council members remained at Jamestown: John Smith, John Ratcliffe, and Matthew Scrivener. Council member Captain John Martin took the opportunity to return to England aboard the *Phoenix*. Having restored peace, and with the fort in reasonable condition and crops in the field, Smith felt it time to undertake a voyage to explore the Chesapeake Bay and its tributaries. He and fourteen other men sailed the barge.

This first voyage of discovery concentrated on the eastern shore of the bay and lasted about two weeks. During that voyage, the men named many prominent sites, starting with Smith's Island near Cape Charles. Names of Smith's friends and relatives dot the map of the region, including Point Ployer, named for Smith's friend in Brittany, and Rickard's Cliffs, in honor of Smith's mother's family.

Smith and his companions sailed about twelve miles above the mouth of the Patapsco River (at present-day Baltimore, Maryland) before a combination of illness and unfavorable weather forced them back toward Jamestown. By June 16, they had reached the mouth of the broad Potomac River and could not resist venturing about thirty miles up that waterway. Near Nomini Bay on the Virginia shore, several hundred Native Americans surrounded the barge. Smith fired his guns, and the Native Americans dropped their weapons. When he spoke with them, they said that Powhatan, urged on by malcontents at Jamestown, had ordered the Native Americans to attack Smith and his companions.

Smith learned that the river he was on was called the Potomac. Rumors Smith and Newport had heard from the natives led him to believe that gold or silver could be found there. Smith and his crew decided to press on upriver and sailed as far as the channel allowed, reaching the undistinguished site of mud flats that one day would become Washington, DC. They actually sailed about six miles north of the present District of Columbia to the rocky falls, where Smith found yellow deposits that he thought might be valuable. He probably had found gold but did not realize it.

Although Smith's exploration did not find a conventional gold mine, his report of the diverse animal skins he saw—wildcat, mink, otter—would spur a rush to exploit them by the London sponsors. He also reported a vast fishing opportunity in the Potomac River and Chesapeake Bay.

On the trip back to Jamestown, Smith wanted to see the Rappahannock River, and it was there that he experienced one of his least pleasant fishing expeditions. He speared a skate—also called a stingray—and when he brought the fish on board, the skate lashed Smith with its barbed tail. Within a few hours Smith's arm had swollen enormously, and his crew expected him to die. However, their physician, Dr. Walter Russell, treated the wound with medicinal oil, and by evening, Smith began to improve. He was sufficiently well, in fact, to eat the skate he had caught. The map of their voyage identifies the spot where Smith encountered the skate as Stingray Point.

When the explorers arrived back at Jamestown on July 21, they found that the colonists who had arrived on Newport's resupply ship had fallen sick. Also, President Ratcliffe had alienated the colonists with his pomposity, his squandering of the supplies, and his insistence on having them build a "palace" for his residence. Hearing Smith's crew report their successful voyage around the Chesapeake and seeing the furs and other prizes they returned with, the colonists called for Ratcliffe's ouster and insisted that John Smith be their president.

With Matthew Scrivener's support, Smith should have had the position of president, but Ratcliffe had two votes according to the Virginia Company articles. This caused a deadlock and an interim period in which Scrivener became the acting president. Ratcliffe's term as president would expire in a couple of months.

Smith was eager to resume his explorations. He wanted to find the fabled route to the Pacific. On July 24, 1608, Smith sailed with a crew of twelve men. He knew he must complete this voyage and return to Jamestown when Ratcliffe's term expired on September 10, otherwise political chaos would reign again in the settlement.

Their route this time took Smith and his men up the western shore of the Chesapeake Bay, and they soon passed the northernmost point of their first voyage. By the time they neared the head of the bay, most of the crew were sick—the English suffered from typhoid fever and dysentery, while introducing the native population to small pox, influenza, measles, and other deadly diseases. As the weakened colonists sailed east across the bay, they ran into a party of eight canoes of Massawomeke, fierce warriors who terrorized the tidewater tribes.

Smith knew they could not outrun the canoes so he boldly sailed right up to them. He hid the sick men under a canvas cover and had their hats put up on sticks as a subterfuge. A man with a musket stood between pairs of the empty hats. The sight of muskets caused the Native Americans to retreat to shore. But Smith sailed up to the canoes and persuaded two of the warriors to come aboard, where they exchanged bells and trinkets for bear meat, venison, fish, and animal pelts.

From their birch-bark canoes and weaponry, Smith recognized that they did not belong to Powhatan's tribes.

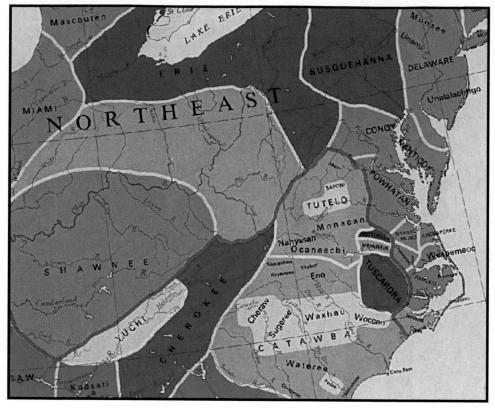

This map, published by the Smithsonian Institution, shows the various tribal regions of early colonial America's Native-American population. (Courtesy of the University of Texas Libraries, The University of Texas at Austin.)

Likewise, Smith's knowledge of the tidewater dialects proved worthless in his attempt to converse with these warriors. They had to communicate via sign language.

Sailing down the eastern shore of the bay the next day, Smith and his crew encountered armed Native Americans in dugout canoes. This group he could talk to, and when he showed them the Massawomeke shields he had obtained in trade, he received a warm welcome. These Nanticoke Indians took the explorers to their village and entertained them. In the village, Smith saw that the Nanticokes had iron implements that did not exist in

Powhatan's domain. They said they had obtained them in trade from the Susquehannocks, who lived up the main branch of the Chesapeake. Smith immediately arranged for a Nanticoke guide and interpreter to take him and his crew up the Susquehannock branch—a trip of about twenty-five miles. In the vicinity of modern-day Havre de Grace, Maryland, Smith waited several days for the Susquehannocks to arrive. Sixty warriors led by several chiefs appeared. They stood quite tall—like giants according to Smith. They brought tobacco pipes with them, as well as gifts of food, baskets, shields, and weapons.

Five Susquehannock chiefs boarded the barge and sailed with the Englishmen back to the Nanticoke village. There the interpreters regaled the chiefs with exaggerated tales of Smith's conquest of the Massawomekes, their common enemy.

The Susquehannocks were greatly impressed. They showered Smith with gifts of painted bearskins, large chains of beads, animal pelts, and other gifts. They wanted Smith to stay and lead an expedition against their enemies, but Smith demurred. He said he had more pressing business, but he would return later to help them. Smith interrogated the chiefs about what bodies of water and tribes dwelt to the north. He surmised from what they told him that a large bay or lake lay to the north. Smith thought that perhaps they referred to the St. Lawrence River in Canada but clearly not the Pacific Ocean. He also considered as evidence of this the iron and brass implements he had seen that he thought had come from the French traders in Canada. The French had been making voyages to Canada since 1524 and actively exploring since at least 1603. Fishermen and traders from various regions of Europe had maintained contact with the Native Americans of the northeast for decades. Smith would have known of France's competing interest in the settlement of North America.

Smith named the most prominent hill visible from the head of the bay Peregrine's Mount in honor of his friend, Lord Willoughby. On the return voyage, he and his crew explored the Patuxent River, where the Native Americans appeared friendly. They bypassed the Potomac and turned northwest to explore the Rappahannock River.

There, the Rappahannock lured them ashore with the prospect of trade. They exchanged hostages—Anas Todkill went ashore as the English representative. Todkill soon saw a group of about two hundred natives waiting to ambush the English. He attempted to get away to alert Smith to the trap. At that, the Native-American hostage jumped overboard and began to swim for shore, but one of Smith's crew shot him, and he died in the water.

Arrows began to fly toward the men in the barge. Todkill, caught in the cross fire, wisely hit the ground. The arrows failed to injure the men on the barge because Smith, as a precaution against such an attack, had fastened shields along the gunwale of the barge forming a

Opposite: *This early-1600s hand-colored woodcut shows an encounter between Smith and a group of Native Americans during his exploration of the Chesapeake.* (Courtesy of the North Wind Picture Archive.)

defensive curtain. Behind the shields, Smith's men fired their muskets at the Rappahannocks with great effect. They soon fled into the forest.

Todkill made a dash for the water and the barge, which Smith had brought close to the shore during the engagement. On shore they found a few dead Native Americans but no wounded. On board the barge, Smith had a most peculiar native guide, named Mosco. This man had a full black beard—highly unusual for Native Americans, who normally had little facial hair. Smith surmised that Mosco must have been descended from a Frenchman. Mosco had sought out the English when he saw them at the mouth of the river; he assumed that they must be related since they also had full beards. Mosco proved to be an excellent judge of how the various tribes in the region would react to the English presence in their river valley. He had warned Smith about the Rappahannocks, and Smith gave Mosco some of their arrows and canoes as a reward.

The farthest Smith's expedition reached was several miles below modern-day Fredericksburg, Virginia. Proceeding on foot, the group encountered another hostile band of natives and found their muskets ineffective in combat in the woods. However, Mosco used his bow and arrows to good advantage, and the skirmish lasted only about thirty minutes. Smith's group took one prisoner, who told Smith through Mosco that the Native Americans believed the English had come to take their country from them.

That evening, back in the barge, Smith and his crew endured another attack. Seeing how effective the shields had been, Smith encircled the entire barge with a curtain of shields. Flights of arrows arced toward the barge from the shore, but to no effect. When day broke, Smith had the shields lowered and presented an unarmed stance to the natives on shore. He offered to trade peacefully. He learned that their tribe was called the Manahoacs, and eventually they put their weapons down and welcomed Smith and his men to their land. They exchanged presents, and Smith left behind an estimated four hundred newly friendly Native Americans as he sailed down the Rappahannock River.

Before Smith left the river, he had one last encounter, this time with the Rappahannocks and their enemies, the Moraughtacunds, who generally waged war across the divide of the river. This time, Smith brought the two tribes together and negotiated peace between them. They gave Smith and his crew a rousing send-off the next day after an evening of feasting and celebrations.

Smith received good and bad news on landing. Matthew Scrivener still had control as acting president, and Ratcliffe was under arrest for mutiny, but more colonists had died and bad weather had spoiled some of the supplies from England. However, their attempt at agriculture had produced a good crop.

As expected, on September 10, 1608, John Smith became president of the English colony in America. He wasted no time redirecting the colonists on important tasks to improve the security of the settlement. They strengthened the fort, fixed the leaking roof on the storehouse, and repaired the church. Smith also imposed discipline on the men: they drilled to become more effective in battle.

Spurred on by Smith's letter and map, the London sponsors accelerated preparations for a resupply voyage to Virginia. Newport sailed for America, and by the end of September, his ship, the *Mary and Margaret*, entered the James River. Seventy new colonists arrived with Newport, including the first two English women to arrive in the new colony.

Newport and Smith were at odds from the start. Newport brought a letter from the Council of Virginia (the Virginia Company's governing body in London) telling Smith that he must submit to Newport's verbal instructions. Newport reiterated the same three priorities from the sponsors: find gold, find the survivors from the Roanoke venture, and find the passage to the Pacific Ocean. Smith, of course, had other priorities—all calculated to put the struggling settlement on a positive and permanent course. By now, Smith would have doubted the existence of gold or a passage to the Pacific.

But the height of folly, in Smith's opinion, was the Virginia Company's instruction to crown Powhatan as emperor of all the tribes in an English coronation ceremony. Smith would never have advocated elevating

Opposite: *A nineteenth-century lithograph of Captain John Smith.* (Courtesy of the Granger Collection.)

that most dangerous opponent's status. However, Captain Newport insisted on carrying out their orders.

To retain some control, Smith convinced Newport to let him invite Powhatan to come to Jamestown for the coronation rather than perform the ceremony at Werowocomoco in front of Powhatan's subjects. Newport agreed, and Smith set out to Werowocomoco with a party of four or five men, showing how confident he had become of his safety with Powhatan. When they arrived, they learned that Powhatan was away but expected back in the village soon.

As they prepared to spend the night in the village, they heard a loud commotion, and out of the woods came about thirty nearly naked women, with painted bodies, wearing deer antlers on their heads. Their leader was none other than Pocahontas, who had arranged this impromptu surprise in honor of the return of her good friend, John Smith. The women entertained them by dancing around the fire and singing. A banquet accompanied by more singing and dancing concluded the formal ceremonies.

When Powhatan arrived the next day, he dismissed all of Smith's suggestions. He insisted that Newport come to Werowocomoco. Smith, as part of his introduction of Newport's proposal, had said that the English planned to continue up the James River and to vanquish Powhatan's enemies, the Monacans, who lived in the mountains to the west. Powhatan informed Smith that he felt perfectly capable of defeating the Monacans. He also told Smith that there was no ocean beyond the mountains, insisting he would know if there were.

Smith returned to Jamestown and assisted Newport in making the preparations for the coronation trip back to Werowocomoco. Newport traveled overland with fifty musketeers while Smith sailed, the boat laden with presents from the Virginia Company, eighty miles to Werowocomoco on the York River.

A day later, with pomp and ceremony bearing little resemblance to an actual English coronation, Powhatan received a copper crown, a scarlet robe, and many other presents. Powhatan gave Newport his old moccasins and his deerskin cape.

As Smith feared, the coronation had a negative effect on the relations between the English and the natives. Powhatan now looked down on the English as his subjects. Perhaps naively, the Virginia Company had expected that their ceremony would have made Powhatan feel subservient to King James and to the king's representatives: Smith and Newport. Far from it. Powhatan sent Smith and Newport back to Jamestown with only a few baskets of corn and, grudgingly, one native guide for their planned expedition up the James River.

Back in Jamestown, Newport took 120 of the fittest men and journeyed up the James in search of gold and the passage to the Pacific. Smith remained in Jamestown with about eighty sickly men tasked to saw and split clapboards to load in the ship's cargo hold. Smith fumed at this blow to his ego. After all, he had much more experience in exploring this country. But Smith swallowed his pride and applied himself to the assigned work.

Meanwhile, Newport found that the disassembled barge he had taken was too heavy for the men to carry. So, they moored their ship and proceeded upstream on foot into the Monacan territory. Newport's expedition didn't go far—perhaps fifty miles. They found what they thought was silver in one mine and retreated to the falls. Attempts to barter for food proved fruitless, and so the great expedition returned to Jamestown with nothing to show for their efforts.

Smith quickly put the healthier men to work on more productive tasks: making glass, tar, and soap ashes, among other supplies. The fall of 1608 passed uneventfully. Newport set sail in December, taking with him Ratcliffe and two documents from John Smith: a letter to the King's Council for Virginia, and his *Map of Chesapeake Bay and the Rivers.*

With Newport's departure, food again became the central issue. Smith had nearly 180 people to feed, and Newport had sailed away with three barrels of the colony's precious provisions to sustain his crew on the Atlantic crossing. Smith looked to the Native Americans to provide food and soon found that Powhatan had instructed the weroances not to assist the English—he apparently planned to starve them out of his land. Smith learned this distressing news when he visited the Nansemonds, where he expected to trade for four hundred baskets of corn, but they refused.

What Smith could not get peacefully he would take by force. He made this clear at Nansemond, where he led an attack. He felt he had little choice—winter would soon prevent commerce with the Native Americans, and the colonists would surely not survive without adequate rations. Consequently, he forced the Nansemond not only to fill his boats but also to promise to plant corn in the spring and reserve it for the English. This approach again put Smith in conflict with the Virginia Company's policy regarding the Native Americans. Smith told the council he wanted to take the problem directly to Powhatan by invading his seat of power at Werowocomoco, but the other council members refused.

Then a strange request from Powhatan shifted the whole dispute. Powhatan offered corn in exchange for swords, muskets, chickens, and an English-style house to be built at Werowocomoco for his residence. The invitation turned out to be an elaborate plot to lure Smith to Werowocomoco and assassinate him, at least according to one friendly Native American Smith consulted.

Nonetheless, Smith decided to take Powhatan's challenge. He led his expedition, in several boats, through ice-clogged waters, arriving at Werowocomoco on January 12, 1609. Powhatan and Smith sparred verbally for days. Smith would build the house, but he would not arm Powhatan with English weapons. Furthermore, he would not come into Werowocomoco without an armed escort. Finally, Powhatan withdrew into the woods, and some of his men attempted to isolate Smith from his musketeers. Smith, as usual, responded boldly and with force. Some

Overleaf: *John Smith's map of Virginia and the Chesapeake Bay region.* (Library of Congress)

of the natives were wounded in the skirmish. But Powhatan, emerging from the woods, insisted that the conflict had all been an unfortunate mistake. He finally directed his people to load the English boats with corn. Once the boats were loaded, they were mired in the mud at low tide. They had to spend the night in that precarious condition, and Powhatan planned to take the opportunity to eliminate the English while they were most vulnerable. But Pocahontas came to Smith and warned him of her father's treachery, putting her own life at risk by doing so.

Smith sailed away from Werowocomoco, Pocahontas, and Powhatan for the last time. However, Powhatan continued to stand strong against the encroaching colonists. Smith had left several Dutch carpenters at the village to build Powhatan's English-style house. Powhatan convinced them to come over to his side. He instructed them to steal English weapons and to attempt to bring some of the other colonists into the plot. He made a compelling offer: come over to the Native American side and have plenty to eat, or stay at Jamestown, starve, and await the Indian massacre of the colonists.

Meanwhile, Smith and his fleet sailed to Opechancanough's village to obtain more food for the colony. Again, as directed by Powhatan, Opechancanough tried to assassinate Smith, but Smith stood his ground, outmaneuvered and out-bluffed his foes, and made his escape. At one point, Smith and several English companions ate food laced with a special poison the natives had gone to great lengths to obtain. But the poison merely made them vomit as soon as they ate it, and it had no permanent effect.

Smith returned to Jamestown by the end of February 1609 with adequate supplies for the colonists. In his absence, his ally Scrivener and several others had drowned when their boat overturned in a storm on the James River. Smith found he was the sole council member remaining.

Inexplicably, the colonists seemed to be content to sit and wait for the Native Americans to bring them corn and for resupply ships from England to replenish their stores. Smith was among the few with enough pluck to do whatever work necessary. Some of the artisans among them did test the sand for its glassmaking qualities; they did some construction within the fort and made some attempt at growing corn. But John Smith clearly felt that their efforts were woefully inadequate to guarantee the survival of the colony, and he knew that they could not just wait for the next supply from England. Appalled at the idleness of the colonists, he called them all to an assembly and pronounced, "He that will not work, shall not eat." No one could doubt that John Smith would carry out this edict. Many of them could testify firsthand to Smith's tenacity.

With John Smith in charge, settlers made many improvements at Jamestown, including a new well and a blockhouse. Also, the colonists amassed stockpiles of glass, tar, and clapboards for eventual shipment to England.

Likewise, agriculture expanded to thirty acres of corn, three sows brought in 1608 had produced a herd of sixty pigs, and the chickens now numbered about five hundred.

But the plotting by Powhatan and the Dutchmen continued to disturb the equilibrium at Jamestown, and a second, unsuccessful attempt to displace John Smith had to be deflected. Added to this, much of the food stores became inedible and rat-infested. Smith dispersed some colonists to fend for themselves downriver. Some others he sent to live with friendly Native Americans. Finally, relief and hope arrived in early July 1609 in the form of one ship commanded by Samuel Argall.

Argall reported that additional relief should arrive soon, as other ships were being loaded when he sailed from Portsmouth. There was a new, shorter route to Virginia that replaced the long voyage from the Canaries south to the West Indies, instead sailing west toward the mid-Atlantic coast. The promised relief ships began arriving in mid-August. This third resupply effort, in 1609, consisting of nine ships loaded with about five hundred new colonists and supplies, represented a major shift in the Virginia Company's approach to the New World. To Smith's chagrin, they also brought news that the old Virginia Company charter had been replaced by a new one, essentially creating a private enterprise, greatly expanded and with a new form of governance. By this time, the Virginia Company recognized, in part due to correspondence from Smith and others, that the sporadic approach they had taken was not working. From the same sources, they also realized that rule-by-committee in Virginia had not been successful. A new streamlined approach to local governance of the colony was intended to eliminate the bickering and factionalism that had impeded the colony for the first three years. The sponsors had chosen to eliminate rule by a council in favor of rule by one appointed governor. This governor, Lord De La Warr, would have full authority and accountability for the day-to-day conduct of the colony in Virginia. Until the governor's arrival, his deputy, Sir Thomas Gates, would take charge.

But the ship carrying Sir Thomas Gates and the written instructions from the new Virginia Company did not arrive at Jamestown. It shipwrecked at Bermuda. This news arrived a couple of weeks later, as the four remaining battered ships finally came to Jamestown. Smith refused to yield his presidency in the absence of written instructions. In late August, two more ships arrived, one with Smith's old nemesis, Captain Ratcliffe. Once again, politics divided the colonists, some insisting that Smith step down and others equally insistent that he remain as president. The anti-Smith faction finally put forward Francis West, Lord De La Warr's brother, as acting governor, but with instructions not to interfere with Smith until his term expired.

About three hundred colonists now crowded into Jamestown. Smith, for his part, continued to make plans for the winter by dispersing some of the colonists downriver and attempting to reestablish trade, as well as bringing in their own harvest.

Another group had gone up the James River to start a new settlement there under the command of Francis West. Smith passed West sailing downriver as he sailed upriver to visit that site. What Smith found displeased him. He felt the site West had chosen would be prone to flooding and would not be as defensible as a site on a hill nearby. Smith bargained with local natives, who had a village on the hill, and soon had bought the village for the English.

However, the English settlers, in a bizarre twist, objected to the move and drew their weapons against John Smith. Smith withdrew in disgust. As soon as he left, some of the Native Americans attacked the settlers, killing many of them. Smith heard the commotion and returned to the settlers' aid. He took command and put those who objected to his leadership in irons. Then he moved the settlers to the village on the hill, where they remained until Francis West returned. West objected to Smith's interference, and Smith decided to let him have his way. Soon, the settlers had moved all of their possessions out of the village and back down the hill to their flood-prone campsite. Disgusted, Smith boarded his boat and sailed downstream toward Jamestown.

Smith fell asleep in the barge during the seventy-five mile journey. As he slept, a spark from someone's pipe or musket fuse ignited a powder bag laying in his lap. Awakened by the flames and in agonizing pain, Smith leapt overboard. His men pulled Smith back into the barge and did what they could to ease the pain of his severe burns.

Back in Jamestown, Smith's agony kept him in bed, and some of his foes even attempted to induce one of the colonists to assassinate him. However, the would-be assassin lost his nerve. When Smith learned of this latest mess, he resolved the leadership crisis by arranging for his own passage back to England.

The plotters, after much difficulty, selected George Percy to be their president. As it turned out, Smith's ship sailed on or near the date his presidency would have expired legally—September 10, 1609. Smith's spirits as well as his health were understandably low on the two-month voyage back home. He would not learn until he returned to London that the sponsors still held him in high regard.

Smith amassed a large volume of geographical and ethnological information on his two voyages. His failure to find a passage to the Pacific Ocean or to find gold may have left him disappointed, but what he did find would be invaluable for future explorers, historians, and anthropologists.

ten

TELLING
HIS STORY

With Smith in low spirits, rejected by the leaders at Jamestown after all he had done to keep the fragile enterprise alive, the seven-week voyage back to England was a test of endurance. Many times in Virginia, the precious flame of the English hopes had nearly died, only to be fanned back to life by John Smith's strong will and clear vision. When the twenty-nine-year-old Englishman reached London in late November or early December of 1609 and met with the sponsors, he learned that they had named him as the defender of the Jamestown colony and appointed him to the newly formed Governor's Council.

Had he stayed in Jamestown, he would have had the job that he was most suited to given his military experience, his understanding of the Native Americans, and his skill in balancing force and diplomacy in his dealings with them. But John Smith's injury and the absence of the written instructions from London ended any chance for him to achieve those dreams. However, Smith had the gratification of knowing that his contributions had not gone unnoticed. Kept in England by his injury and the turn of events in the Virginia Company, Smith applied pen to paper and began to compile his account of the history of the English colonial experiment in Virginia.

Smith never went back to Jamestown. He had decided that a fresh start in the area north of that colony would be a better opportunity. There, with backing from new investors, John Smith had hoped to develop a new colony using his knowledge of the local conditions and learning from his experience in Jamestown. Had he been successful in getting sustained backing for this new approach, his colony would have undoubtedly avoided the pitfalls that beset Jamestown. Given Smith's background, it is likely that he would have taken farmers, carpenters, fishermen, and other artisans. He would also have installed a more structured command for the local governance of the colony.

John Smith did, in 1614, make a successful voyage to what is now New England. He achieved his goals of mapping the coast and scouting for suitable settlement locations, but made no attempt to establish a permanent colony there, since his voyage had not been equipped to do so. He returned to England with a hold full of valuable salted fish, his maps, and the enthusiasm to launch a colonial attempt on the next voyage.

But his second voyage failed due to inclement weather, and on a third attempt, pirates attacked Smith's ship. As it happened, the pirates knew John Smith from his early years as a mercenary soldier, and they sailed away. However, his good fortune turned when two French pirate ships also overtook them. By this time, some in Smith's crew had grown mutinous because of their captain's stubborn determination to continue on in the face of such poor circumstances. While Smith was on board one of the French ships negotiating the return of

Smith escaped from his French captors during a storm in October of 1615. He is portrayed making his way back to land in the background of this picture. (Library of Congress)

some equipment, his crew abandoned him for a return to England. Smith spent the next several months on board the French ship writing one of his histories of the New World explorations. He eventually escaped off the coast of France and rowed ashore in one of the ship's boats, taking his manuscript with him.

The historical record Smith left in the numerous books he wrote represents an important contribution to posterity. He is, of course, popularly remembered for his capture by Powhatan and his release thanks to the intercession of Powahatan's daughter, Pocahontas. Smith reported this event at least as early as 1616 in a letter to the queen. His admitting that he owed his life to a young Native-American girl does him great credit and belies the reputation of braggart some ascribe to him.

John Smith wrote of his early life and his adventures in Europe, Asia, North Africa, and his last account of his time in America about twenty-five years after the events occurred, near the end of his life. Consequently, his accounts include a few forgivable instances of confusion over geography, misuse of some foreign words, or other lapses in memory. He had experienced more in his short life than most ever will. As to geography, Smith ably made note of all the major rivers, the breadth and extent of the bay, and compiled a comprehensive and surprisingly accurate map of the area, showing not only the geographic features but also the settlements of the native population, their tribal names, and their names for geographic features. Republished under various

Pocahontas is brought before the court of James I during her visit to England with her husband, John Rolfe. (Library of Congress)

mapmakers' names, John Smith's map of the Chesapeake Bay region would serve as the standard for many years.

In 1616, Pocahontas, now known as Rebecca Rolfe, wife of tobacco planter John Rolfe, came to England. She was received as a princess, representing her people in Queen Anne's court. Although John Smith knew she had come to England, he did not immediately seek a meeting with her. Instead, Pocahontas invited Smith to see her.

They met in a drawing room at Brentford near London. Pocahontas, overwhelmed by emotion, turned away to regain her composure. When she had last seen Smith, she was a precocious young girl, actively assisting the English colony. Now, in their final meeting, she was a young wife and mother, and Smith was a thirty-six-year-old bachelor.

Once she brought her emotions in check, Pocahontas told Smith she had been informed that he had died as a result of wounds he received in Virginia. Her father had believed that, as had all of her people. She told Smith she was shocked to learn that he was alive and well in London. She chided him for not coming to see her sooner. She told Smith she looked on him as her father and wanted him to think of her as his child. Smith said she was a king's daughter and he was unworthy of her honor. However, she insisted that she revered him as her father.

Smith and Pocahontas must have wondered how their paths had so diverged after their tumultuous meeting in Powhatan's longhouse in Virginia. After Smith had sailed back to England in 1609, Pocahontas married Kocoum, a Native-American warrior of high rank. Later, the English captured her and held her for ransom at Jamestown. Following her capture, she was christened, taking the name Rebecca, and she married John Rolfe on April 5, 1614. They had one son, Thomas, who accompanied them on their voyage to England.

John Smith would not see her again. Not long after their meeting, Pocahontas fell ill from an unknown malady and died in the spring of 1617 while waiting to sail back to Virginia. She was buried at St. George's Church, Gravesend, England, on March 21, 1617. A statue honoring Pocahontas stands in the churchyard,

This engraving of Pocahontas, at age twenty-one, is the only known image of her made during her lifetime. (The British Museum, London)

and a duplicate stands near the church at Jamestown.

Smith spent the rest of his years living in London,

The Mayflower *made landfall at Plymouth, Massachusetts, in the winter of* *1620.* (Library of Congress)

lodging with friends. In 1620, he was nearly picked to lead the colonists to the Plymouth settlement, but instead the Pilgrims selected Miles Standish to head their expedition to New England. However, they did buy and make use of Smith's maps and books. He continued to write and to meet with potential investors, promoting the idea of settlements in New England.

John Smith devoted his final years to writing, producing nearly a dozen works, including his histories, his memoir, *True Travels,* information for mariners, important maps, and propaganda pieces intended to encourage colonization of the New World. He also compiled the first dictionary of English nautical terms. Though Smith never got another chance to take part in a voyage to the New World, ships sailed regularly to New England on fishing expeditions and conducted explorations of the territory. Once the Plymouth settlement proved successful, England had two important anchors set in America: Virginia and New England. They would go on from there to challenge the French in Canada and develop other colonies in the Mid-Atlantic region. After more than one hundred years lagging behind the Spanish in the Americas, England was well on its way to dominating the North American continent. While John Smith was no longer a direct participant in these activities, his work in England helped keep interest alive in the prospects for wealth offered by the New World.

At the age of fifty-one, Captain John Smith died on June 21, 1631, and was buried at St. Sepulchre's-Without-Newgate Church in London. According to Smith's will, he still owned houses and land in Lincolnshire. The Ashmolean Museum in Oxford, England, houses a number of artifacts that may have been collected by Smith over the course of his adventures, including Powhatan's cloak.

Throughout his life, Smith exhibited a high sense of honor, incredible fortitude, bravery, and a clear focus on his goals. His ability to communicate effectively with many different cultures in all the diverse languages he encountered indicates Smith had great intelligence. He

John Smith's coat of arms can be found immortalized in stained glass at St. Helena's church in his hometown of Willoughby. (Courtesy of Aleck Loker.)

created some of the best maps of the east coast of North America—used by explorers and colonists who came after him and reprinted for many years with only minor changes.

He also recorded important ethnological information about the Native Americans he encountered. However, John Smith contributed much more to America. His strong personality, his determination, and his skill in dealing with foreign cultures provided the bond that held together England's first permanent settlement in America.

TIMELINE

1580   John Smith is baptized on January 9 (exact date of birth unknown).

1595   Apprenticed to a merchant in King's Lynn, sixty miles from home.

1596   Smith's father dies; Smith travels to the Netherlands and joins the English army fighting the Spanish there.

1599   Travels to France and Scotland.

1600   Goes abroad again to fight for the Holy Roman Empire against the Turks.

1601   Participates in the siege of Olumpagh, capture of Alba Regalis, and battle of Charka Gorge.

1602   Smith is captured in battle.

1603   Sold as a slave and sent to Constantinople; escapes that fall.

1604   Travels through Germany, France, Spain, and Africa; returns to England.

1605   Involved in planning an expedition to Virginia.

1606   Sails for America from London aboard *Susan Constant* on December 19.

1607   Restrained as a prisoner during the voyage; makes landfall at the Chesapeake Bay on April 26; arrives at Jamestown on May 13; captured by Native Americans in December.

1608	Makes two voyages of discovery around the Chesapeake Bay; made president of the colony on September 10.
1609	Wounded in an accident; returns to England.
1614	Makes a second voyage to America.
1616	Reunited with Pocahontas during her visit to England.
1617	Pocahontas dies.
1618	Powhatan dies.
1631	John Smith dies on June 21.

Sources

CHAPTER ONE: Born to Escape

p. 18, "Age of Exploration..." Sarah Flowers, *The Age of Exploration,* World History Series (San Diego, CA: Lucent Books, 1999), 13.

p. 18, "lost colony," David B. Quinn, *Set Fair for Roanoke, Voyages and Colonies, 1584-1606* (Chapel Hill: University of North Carolina Press, 1985), xvi.

CHAPTER TWO: First Taste of Adventure

p. 27, "Let no act . . ." Marcelus Aurelius, *Meditations* (Mineola, NY: Dover Publications, 1997), 19.

p. 29, "Depreau," John Smith, *The Complete Works,* vol. 3, ed. Philip Barbour (Chapel Hill: University of North Carolina Press, 1986), 158.

p. 31, "a rabble of inhuman . . ." Smith, *The Complete Works,* vol. 3, 159.

CHAPTER THREE: The Holy Wars

p. 46, "made his valor shine . . ." Smith, *The Complete Works,* vol. 3, 168.

p. 46, "it was a terror . . ." Ibid., 168.

CHAPTER FOUR: Battle Worn, Battle Ready

p. 50, "vampire," Raymond T. McNally and Radu Florescu, *In Search of Dracula, The History of Dracula and Vampires, Completely Revised* (Boston: Houghton Mifflin Company, 1994), 126, 130.

p. 51, "You laugh at me . . ." Andrei Codrescu, *The Blood Countess* (New York: Dell Publishing, 1995), 389.

p. 53, "Plain of Regall," Smith, *The Complete Works,* vol. 3, 171.

p. 55, "to delight the ladies," Ibid., 172.

p. 56, "Grualgo," Ibid., 173.

p. 57, "servants," Ibid., 173.

p. 57, "Bonny Mulgro," Ibid., 173.

p. 64, "German," Smith, *The Complete Works,* vol. 3, 180.

CHAPTER FIVE: Life in Captivity

p. 67, "Girl from Trabzon," Barbour, *The Complete Works,* vol. 3, 186 (in Note 2).

p. 69, "noble gentlewoman," Smith, *The Complete Works,* vol. 3, 187.

p. 69, "adorn her . . ." Ibid., 187.

p. 70, "Nalbrits," Ibid.

p. 70, "Cambia," Ibid.

p. 70, "Bruapo River," Ibid., 188.

p. 70, "vast stony castle," Ibid.

p. 70, "tyrannical," Ibid.

p. 71, "till time made her . . ." Ibid.

p. 72, "samboyses and muselbits," Ibid., 189.

p. 72, "coava," Ibid.

p. 73, "God . . . help his servants . . ." Ibid., 200.

p. 74, "beat his brains out," Smith, *The Complete Works,* vol. 3, 200.

p. 76, "good lady," Ibid., 201.

p. 76, "largely supplied . . ." Ibid., 201.

CHAPTER SIX: The New World Beckons

p. 86, "remote heathen and barbarous lands . . ." Quinn, *Set Fair for Roanoke,* 9.

p. 95, "restrained," Smith *The Complete Works,* vol. 1, 206.

CHAPTER SEVEN: Virginia's First Diplomat

p. 97, "nobody," Philip L. Barbour, *The Three Worlds of Captain John Smith* (Boston: Houghton Mifflin Company, 1964), 86.

p. 98, "an oration . . ." Barbour, *Three Worlds,* 125.

p. 104-105, "begged in Ireland . . ." Ibid., 145.

p. 108, "intend[ing] to usurpe . . ." Smith, *The Complete Works,* vol. 1, 207.

p. 116, "two sacrificial stones," Barbour, Three Worlds, 168.

p. 116, "In the utmost . . ." Ibid., 363.

CHAPTER EIGHT: Keeping the Flame Alive

p. 120, "gold," John Smith, *The Complete Works of Captain John Smith,* vol. 2, ed. Philip L. Barbour (Chapel Hill: University of North Carolina Press, 1986), 157.

p. 123, "proffered," Smith, *The Complete Works,* vol. 1, 65.

p. 123, "father," Ibid., 65.

CHAPTER NINE: President and Explorer

p. 134, "palace," Smith, *The Complete Works,* vol. 1, 233.

p. 151, "He that will not work . . ." Smith, *The Complete Works,* vol. 2, 208.

BIBLIOGRAPHY

Aurelius, Marcus. *Meditations.* Mineola, NY: Dover Publications, 1997.

Barbour, Philip L. *The Three Worlds of Captain John Smith.* Boston: Houghton Mifflin Company, 1964.

Codrescu, Andrei. *The Blood Countess.* New York: Dell Publishing, 1995.

Flowers, Sarah. *The Age of Exploration.* World History Series. San Diego, CA: Lucent Books, 1999.

Machiavelli, Niccollò. *The Art of War.* New York: Da Capo Press, 1990.

McNally, Raymond T. and Radu Florescu. *In Search of Dracula: The History of Dracula and Vampires.* Revised edition. Boston: Houghton Mifflin Company, 1994.

Pettigrew, Andrew, Alastair Duke, and Gillian Lewis. *Calvinism in Europe, 1540-1620.* Cambridge, UK: Cambridge University Press, 1994.

Quinn, David B. *Set Fair for Roanoke: Voyages and Colonies, 1584-1606.* Chapel Hill: University of North Carolina Press, 1985.

Smith, John. *The Complete Works of Captain John Smith.* Edited by Philip L. Barbour. 3 vols. Chapel Hill: University of North Carolina Press, 1986.

WEB SITES

http://www.apva.org/history/index.html
The Association for the Preservation of Virginia Antiquities
sponsors the Jamestown archaeological discovery project. The
site includes histories of the figures involved with Jamestown,
a timeline, and a list of settlers with their occupations.

http://www.jamestowne.org/
The Jamestowne Society organizes groups of descendants from
the original pioneers of the Jamestown settlement. The site
documents history and offers a bibliography for other reading.

www.theottomans.org
This site discusses the Ottoman Empire's history, wars, art, and
culture. There are maps, a glossary, and links to other Web sites
that discuss the history-rich territory in and around Turkey.

INDEX

tria), 36-37, 42, 47
Francis I, 39

Gates, Sir Thomas, 153
Gilbert, Bartholomew, 88
Godspeed, 93, *94*
Gosnold, Bartholomew, 88, *89,*
   90-91, 93, 97, 102, 104
Grualgo, 56-57

Hakluyt, Richard, 90-91
Henry IV (king of France), 28
Holy Roman Empire, 38-39,
   62

James VI (of Scotland) and I
   (of England), 25, 93, 128
John I, 42

Kendall, George, 97, 106, 108-
   109
Khissl, Hans Jacob, 36, 39-41
Kocoum, 161

La Roche, Captain, 32, 34-35,
   36, 75
Leo III (pope), 38
de Lorraine, Phillippe-
   Emmanuel (duke of
   Mercoeur), 28-29, *29,* 42-
   48
Lost colony, 87-88, 103, 142

Machiavelli, Niccolò, 25-27,
   26
Martin, John, 97, 102, 106,
   109, 125, 132
Mary and Margaret, 142
Massawomeke, 135-137
Mattaponi, 99
Mayflower, 163
Mehmet III, 45
Meldritch, Earl of, 37, 41-43,
   45-46, 49-50, 52-54, 59-
   61, 65, 67, 77-78
Merham, Captain, 79, 81
Metham, George, 21
Monacan, 146
Moraughtacunds, 141
Mosco, 140-141
Mulgro, 57-59, *58*

Namontack, 125
Nansemonds, 147
Nanticoke, 137
Nelson, Thomas, 120, 127
Newport, Christopher, 90, 93,
   95, 97-103, 106, 120-125,
   121, 142, 144-146

Opechancanough, 112-114,
   130, 150-151

Paleologue, Theodore, 27-28,
   55, 67
Pamunkey, 99, 112-113